Annie Blouin tackles the deep subjects of 'Living for Forever Now' in a skillful weaving of prophetic revelation, heart engagement and wise understanding of scripture. Annie is an anointed teacher and messenger, a true prophetic voice for this time.

                                                -Patricia Bootsma
                                                Sr. Associate Pastor, CTF Toronto
                                                Leader of the CTF Toronto HOP

Practical and interactive! Annie outlines the necessary areas of learning along the journey to mature the gift and call of the prophetic ministry. She teaches clearly on the mindsets and skills needed to successfully navigate the revelation realm and not get sidelined by the enemy. Annie talks honestly about the challenges she has faced and the keys God has taught her as she has developed in her prophetic ministry.

                                                -Lynley Allan
                                                Senior Pastor, CTF Auckland, NZ

In addressing God's heart and ways in the sections of this book, Annie has given us an excellent roadmap to deepening our relationship with the Father, so that we don't run into the same pitfalls the ancient Israelites did. What I love is that this is not just theory, but is revelation, personal stories and practical insight from Annie's own journey of intimacy with God.

                                                -Murray Smith
                                                Lead Pastor, CTF Raleigh/Durham, NC

Prophetic Revelation

Keys to Spiritual Maturity

Annie Blouin

In association with

© Copyright 2018 by Annie Blouin

Published by Life Press Publishing

Knightdale, NC 27545

Printed in the United States of America

ISBN 978-0-9978847-1-5

Religion / Christian Life / Spiritual Growth

$25.00

Books by Annie Blouin are available at:

www.lifepresspublishing.com

www.amazon.com

All rights reserved. This book is protected by the copyright laws of the United States of America. No part of this publication may be reproduced, stored in a retrieval system, or transmitted in any form or by any means without the prior written permission of the publisher. The only exception is brief quotations in printed reviews.

Unless otherwise identified, Scripture quotations are taken from the New King James Version®. Copyright ©1982 by Thomas Nelson, Inc. Used by permission. All rights reserved.

Scripture quotations marked Passion Translation are taken from The Passion Translation®, copyright © 2017. Used by permission of BroadStreet Publishing Group, LLC, Racine, Wisconsin, USA. All rights reserved.

Scripture quotations marked The Amplified Bible are taken from The Amplified Bible, New Testament copyright © 1954, 1958, 1987 by The Lockman Foundation. Used by permission. All rights reserved.

Also by Annie Blouin

Everlasting Doors:

When the Supernatural Penetrates American Politics

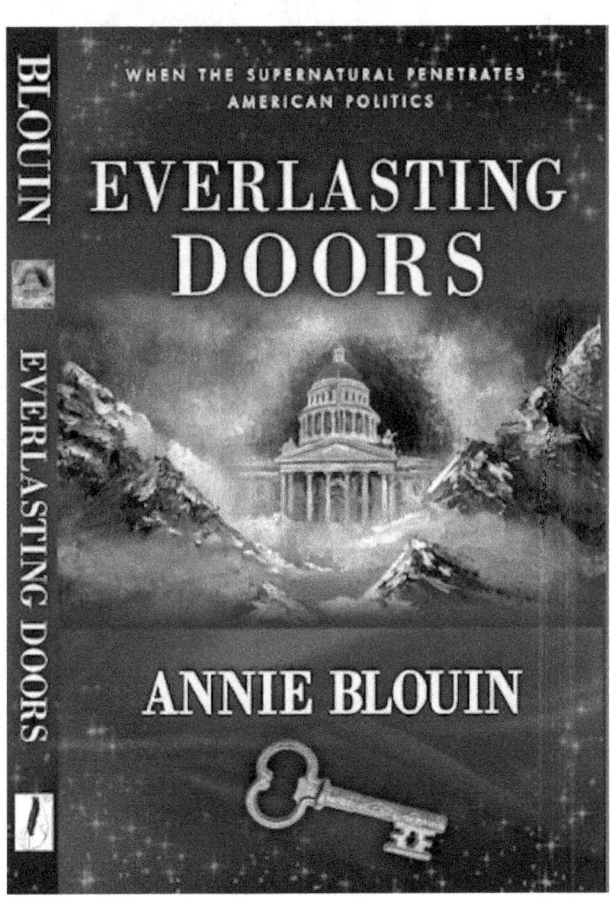

Everlasting Prophetic:

Bridging Heaven to Earth

Annie Blouin

Dedication

This book is dedicated to my husband, Joe. His heart for God, for me, and for our children is unparalleled. Thanks for everything. I love you, for always and forever.

Annie Blouin

Acknowledgements

Thanks to Father God for His unconditional love. You are worth it all.

As with any project, writing a book requires a team effort. I'd like to thank my husband, Joe for his unwavering love and support and for always championing me. I love you for always and forever.

Thanks to my children, Madeleine, Grace, Joey, and Josiah for being patient while I finished this project. I promise I'll cook more dinners now that it is complete. My favorite times are spent with all y'all. I love you guys.

Thanks to CTF Raleigh, a wonderful church family and CTF School of Revival for running passionately after a good Father. Special thanks to Duncan & Kate Smith, Murray & Ash Smith, Aaron & Jacquelyn Mitchell. I love all of you and am thankful for you.

Thanks to Kim, Pamela, Coleen, Jeanine, Cathy, Bryan, JoAnn, Judy, Holly, Christy, Suzanne, and Lauren for helping birth this book in prayer. I couldn't have done it without all of you.

Thanks to Murray for your heart to pursue God and the prophetic. Thanks for all of your input on this book and your heart for anchoring the prophetic in the Word of God. Your willingness and passion to explore the prophetic realm together continues to inspire me.

Thanks to Margaret Cantrell for your professional editing and for your friendship. I'm thankful for you!

Special thanks to Jordan and Adrianne for help with the cover owl. I love his blue eyes!

Annie Blouin

x

Contents

Foreword   13

Introduction   15

God's Heart

Chapter 1   Living for Eternity   17

Chapter 2   Getting Healthy: Spirit, Soul, & Body   29

Chapter 3   Getting Equipped & Competent   57

God's Ways

Chapter 4   Prophetic Journeys with God   73

Chapter 5   Angels   81

Chapter 6   7 Mountains   93

God's Voice

Chapter 7   Scripture! Scripture! Scripture!   99

Chapter 8   Shifting Atmospheres   109

Chapter 9   Next Move of God   121

Annie Blouin

Foreword

God is an incredibly relational Being. He has existed in perfect communion as Father, Son and Holy Spirit for all eternity. He birthed all of creation, and humans as the pinnacle of His creation made in His image, in Love, by Love and for Love. We have been created to enjoy His unfailing love, to live in His goodness and to walk in fellowship with Him. The mission of Jesus through His incarnation, perfect life, death, resurrection, ascension and glorification was to bring us into the glory of being God's sons, so that we can enjoy fullness of fellowship with the Holy Spirit.

God is a master communicator. He speaks to us in many ways through the language of the Spirit. As His sons (which is about our inheritance not our gender) His desire is to speak to us and to reveal His secrets, but because He doesn't always speak to us in English it is vital that we learn to hear His voice. Annie has done an excellent job in laying out the many aspects of God's voice in this book. As a pastor, I particularly love her chapter on the importance of prophetic people being grounded in the truth of scripture.

As well as learning to hear God's voice, we also need to experience more of His heart and ways. One of the primary reasons that the ancient Israelites who came out of Egypt did not enter the land God had promised to give them was because they did not know God's ways (Psalm 95:7-11, Hebrews 3:7-11). They saw God powerfully work on their behalf for over 40 years, lived with God's presence as the pillar of fire and the cloud, and heard God's voice through Moses. Despite all the miracles around them, they didn't inherit the promises as they neither understood God's heart to bless them, nor His ways of using their circumstances to build their faith.

In addressing God's heart and ways in the sections of this book, Annie has given us an excellent roadmap to deepening our relationship with the Father, so that we don't run into the same pitfalls. What I love is that this is not just theory, but is revelation, personal stories and practical insight from Annie's own journey of intimacy with God.

I highly recommend this book to you. It is full of wisdom and revelation, helpful examples from Annie's life, powerful revelation and practical exercises to develop not just your prophetic gift but increase your hunger for more of God. I encourage you to take the time to complete each exercise thoroughly, and let Holy Spirit transform your life.

As you work through the material in the book and listen to Holy Spirit, may He give you eyes to see, ears to hear, and most importantly a heart to understand.

Murray Smith
Lead Pastor
CTF Raleigh/Durham, NC

INTRODUCTION

I fell deeply in love with the Father, Son and Holy Spirit when I was baptized in the Holy Spirit October 6, 2002. I had gotten saved April 13, 1997 when I witnessed the love and power of the Lord but my heart fully awakened in 2002. If you're like me, someone who knew the Lord but didn't feel passionate for Him, ask the Holy Spirit to fill you like He did for the disciples in the Upper Room. His power and love is like a rocket booster to life. Power, purpose and passion come with the Baptism of the Holy Spirit.

My gift for seeing into the supernatural realms opened fully in 2002. It's been a wild ride!

One day during my time with the Lord, He asked me what I wanted from Him. The way He asked reminded me of how He asked Solomon what He wanted. I felt the holiness of the moment. I carefully searched my heart and considered His question. After much thought, I asked the Lord for an anointing on my life that whomever encounters me would develop a great hunger for more of Jesus.

Beloved, I pray that as you read this book, you would encounter the One who loves you beyond measure and hunger for deep intimacy with Him.

Discover, Demonstrate, & Display

God's Heart, God's Ways, & God's Voice

through the Prophetic

God's Heart

CHAPTER 1

LIVING FOR ETERNITY

From the moment that God creates each one of us and sends us to earth into our mother's womb, we begin our journey into eternity forward. He sends us with the blueprints of our unique identity, our purpose and His heart of love for us. Our lives are a journey of discovering what He already put in us, discovering who He is, and living a life worthy of reward. For some of us, we grow up knowing Him and for others it takes decades for us to find our way back to Him. Unfortunately, some live their entire lives without knowing Him.

My son developed verbal skills early and was speaking in full sentences by the time he was 17 months old. One day before he was two years old, as I was holding him on my lap in the rocking chair, he told me that he remembered sitting on God's lap before he came into my tummy. Then he said he missed being with God. His comments astonished me. As he spoke, the Presence of God flooded the room with such love. I searched Scripture to see if we really were with God as He created us and sent us to earth. I didn't find reference to what my son said, but I did find God's heart towards us. "Before I formed you in the womb, I knew you. Before you were born, I set you apart." Jeremiah 1:5.

My favorite verse in the Bible is Zephaniah 3:17, "The Lord your God in your midst, the Mighty One, will save; He will rejoice over you with gladness, He will quiet you with His love, He will rejoice over you with singing." As we consider our lives and what living for eternity comprises, it has to be filtered through the Father's heart of love towards us. He made us from love and for love. Consider the following verses of Scripture and how deeply God loves us.

"The Lord has appeared of old to me, saying: Yes, I have loved you with an everlasting love; Therefore, with loving kindness I have drawn you." Jeremiah 31:3. He's referring to Israel here in this verse, but it expresses His heart of love for all of us.

"We love Him because He first loved us." 1 John 4:19.

Jesus is praying for all believers in John 17:20-23, "I do not pray for these alone, but also for those who will believe in Me through their word; that they all may be one, as You, Father, are in Me, and I in You; that they also may be one in Us, that the world may believe that You sent me. And the glory which You gave Me I have given them, that they may be one just as We are one: I in them, and You in Me; that they may be made perfect in one, and that the world may know that You have sent Me, and have loved them as You have loved Me."

"As the Father loved Me, I also have loved you; abide in my love." John 15:9

God created you uniquely in order to have relationship with you. God desires to have a daily walk with you in relationship. Your journey with Him will ultimately bring you into a place of peace, joy, and love to manifest to other people and change the world around you. The revelation and the exercises in this workbook will help your heart heal in specific instances but it's not just a quick fix. There are dimensions of immediate breakthrough that will occur and other healing that will come as a result of a process as you walk in love with God. The greatest outcome that I pray for you is that you would love God with all of your heart and that love would be shown through deep ongoing intimacy with Him and love for other people.

PRAYER ACTIVATION

Take a few moments and journal here what the Lord shows you about His heart for you personally.

_____
_____
_____
_____
_____
_____
_____
_____
_____
_____
_____
_____
_____
_____

Salvation

", and from Jesus Christ, the faithful witness, the firstborn from the dead, and the ruler over the kings of the earth. To Him who loved us and washed us from our sins in His own blood." Revelation 1:5

Every person ever born on planet Earth, has the choice of accepting Jesus' sacrifice on the cross. When we receive Jesus as our Savior, we then are able to spend eternity in Heaven with God. If we decide not to accept His sacrifice as payment for our sins, we'll spend our eternity in hell. It's the most important choice we'll ever make this side of eternity. John 3:16 illustrates this: "For God so loved the world that He gave His only begotten Son, that whoever believes in Him should not perish but have everlasting life."

Romans 10:9-10 expounds, "that if you confess with your mouth the Lord Jesus and believe in your heart that God raised Him from the dead, you will be saved. For with the heart one believes unto righteousness, and with the mouth confession is made unto salvation."

Jesus said in John 14:6, "I am the way, the truth and the life. No one comes to the Father except through Me."

PRAYER ACTIVATION

In the following space, record your salvation experience. If you've never asked Jesus to forgive you of your sins and become your Savior, today is the day of salvation!

Eternal Reward

The path of salvation is clear. Accept Jesus' death on the Cross in exchange for forgiveness of personal sin. Good works won't earn a place in Heaven with God just as evil works don't earn eternity in hell. Forgiveness of sin through belief in Jesus is the way to Heaven. That being said, while our belief in Jesus is what determines our eternal destination, how we live our earthly lives determines our heavenly reward. We will all stand before the Judgment seat of God to give an account of our lives. Our receipt of Jesus as our Savior cleanses us of sin and settles the Heaven/Hell issue. We will live our eternal lives with Jesus in Heaven but the reward for our earthly lives is determined by our choices here on earth. The following Scriptures all describe the process of how we receive our eternal reward.

2 Corinthians 5:9-10 explains the Judgment Seat of Christ, "Therefore we make it our aim, whether present or absent, to be well pleasing to Him. For we must all appear before the judgment seat of Christ, that each one may receive the things done in the body, according to what he has done, whether good or bad."

Jesus tells us in Matthew 16:24-27, "Then Jesus said to His disciples, 'If anyone desires to come after Me, let him deny himself, and take up his cross, and follow Me. For whoever desires to save his life will lose it, but whoever loses his life for My sake will find it. For what profit is it to a man if he gains the whole world, and loses his own soul? Or what will a man give in exchange for his soul? For the Son of Man will come in the glory of His Father with His angels, and then He will reward each according to his works."

Hebrews 11:6: "But without faith it is impossible to please Him, for he who comes to God must believe that He is, and that He is a rewarder of those who diligently seek Him."

Jesus testifies to the Churches in Revelation 22:12-13, "And behold, I am coming quickly, and My reward is with Me, to give every one according to his work. I am the Alpha and the Omega, the Beginning and the End, the First and the Last."

The Apostle Paul tells us in 1 Corinthians 3:5-15, "Who then is Paul, and who is Apollos, but ministers through whom you believed, as the Lord gave to each one? I planted, Apollos watered, but God gave the increase. So then neither he who plants is anything, nor he who waters, but God who gives the increase. Now he who plants and he who waters are one, and each one will receive his own reward according to his own labor. For we are God's fellow workers; you are God's field, you are God's building. According to the grace of God which was given to me, as a wise master builder I have laid the foundation, and another builds on it. But let each one take heed how he builds on it. For no other foundation can anyone lay than that which is laid, which is Jesus Christ. Now if anyone builds on this foundation with gold, silver, precious stones, wood, hay, straw, each one's work will become clear; for the Day will declare it, because it will be revealed by fire; and the fire will test each one's work, of what sort it is. If anyone's work which he has built on it endures, he will receive a reward. If anyone's work is burned, he will suffer loss; but he himself will be saved, yet so as through fire."

2 Timothy 4:7-8: "I have fought the good fight, I have finished the race, I have kept the faith. Finally, there is laid up for me the crown of righteousness, which the Lord, the righteous Judge, will give to me on that Day, and not to me only but also to all who have loved His appearing."

These Scriptures tell us that how we live our lives and the motives behind the work we do are critical components to our eternal reward and how we live for all of eternity. The realization that each one of us will stand before God and give an account of our lives should sober us. We will care very much then and will wish we were diligent while we were on earth. John Bevere and Bill Johnson both preached great messages on the topic of living for eternity at Bethel Church Redding in 2017. I highly suggest listening to the podcasts. (Bill Johnson, *What is Most Important* 7/2/17 and John Bevere, *Steward Your Life for Eternity* 3/12/17).

Jesus gives us clear understanding of our responsibility on this planet in the Parable of the Talents in Matthew 25:14-30. We are to discover who God made us to be in our identity and gifts and be faithful with service. "For the kingdom of heaven is like a man traveling to a far country, who called his own servants and delivered his goods to them. And to one he gave five talents, to another two, and to another one, to each according to his own ability; and immediately he went on a journey. Then he who had received the five talents went and traded with them, and made another five talents. And likewise he who had received two gained two more also. But he who had received one went and dug in the ground, and hid his lord's money. After a long time, the lord of those servants came and settled accounts with them. So he who had received five talents came and brought five other talents, saying, 'Lord, you delivered to me five talents; look, I have gained five more talents besides them.' His lord said to him, 'Well done, good and faithful servant; you were faithful over a few things, I will make you ruler over many things. Enter into the joy of your lord.' He also who had received two talents came and said, 'Lord, you delivered to me two talents; look, I have gained two more talents besides them.' His lord said to him, 'Well done, good and faithful servant; you have been faithful over a few things, I will make you ruler over many things. Enter into the joy of your lord.' Then he who had received the one talent came and said, 'Lord, I knew you to be a hard man, reaping where you have not sown, and gathering where you have not scattered seed. And I was afraid, and went and hid your talent in the ground. Look, there you have what is yours.' But his lord answered and said to him, 'You wicked and lazy servant, you knew that I reap where I have not sown, and gather where I have not scattered seed. So you ought to have deposited my money with the bankers, and at my coming I would have received back my own with interest. Therefore take the talent from him, and give it to him who has ten talents. For to everyone who has, more will be given, and he will have abundance; but from him who does not have, even what he has will be taken away. And cast the unprofitable servant into the outer darkness. There will be weeping and gnashing of teeth.'"

Notice in the above passage that people are given different gifts and are responsible for stewarding them. People are created equal in rights, equal in love from God, but not equal in ability or call or favor. The Kingdom of God is not socialistic or communistic. God gives to people in different measures and expects return on His investment. The servant who was given one talent and hid it because he was afraid was not coddled by the Lord. Instead, the Lord called him a wicked and lazy servant. We would do well to understand this principal from a governmental standpoint that while we provide safety nets for people in financial need that we don't handicap and rob them of their ability to grow and be faithful with their God given talents and responsibilities.

Stewards of the Mysteries of God

Fortunately, God is the Judge. I'm not the judge, nor are you. 1 Corinthians 4:1-5: "Let a man so consider us, as servants of Christ and stewards of the mysteries of God. Moreover, it is required in stewards that one be found faithful. But with me it is a very small thing that I should be judged by you or by a human court. In fact, I do not even judge myself. For I know of nothing against myself, yet I am not justified by this; but He who judges me is the Lord. Therefore, judge nothing before the time, until the Lord comes, who will both bring to light the hidden things of darkness and reveal the counsels of the hearts. Then each one's praise will come from God."

Your Individual Identity and Purpose

God has made you unique. There is no one exactly like you on the planet. You represent a facet of God that the world needs to see. The prophetic answers the three questions the world is crying out for the answers to: 1. Who is God? 2. Who am I? 3. What is my Purpose? As you journey with God in relationship, He'll show you personally the answers to all three questions. It may not be today, but He is faithful in relationship. If you examine your life and your interests, you'll get glimpses of your purpose. I didn't get saved until I was nearly 26 years old, but growing up I had clues into my individual call. I knew I wanted to be a writer and a teacher and a mom but without God I personally didn't have the context for those callings because my call specifically is to teach and write and mother in the Body of Christ, as well as other places. As you pursue relationship with God, He will show you what your talents are so that you may hear Him say, "Well done, good and faithful servant; you have been faithful over a few things, I will make you ruler over many things. Enter into the joy of your lord." Matthew 25:23.

PRAYER ACTIVATION

Take some time and journal what gifts and talents you already know you carry. Ask the Lord for insight into more talents and the application of those. Purpose in your heart to be faithful in your call.

_____
_____
_____
_____
_____
_____
_____
_____
_____
_____

Over the course of me discovering my purpose, the Lord gave me two questions to ask Him. I believe they're important in understanding your own individual call.

First, it's important to know how much money you're called to steward for the Kingdom in your lifetime. It's hard to be faithful if you don't know who you are. For some, the answer is tens of thousands of dollars. For others, it's hundreds of thousands. For some, it's millions and still others, it's billions.

PRAYER ACTIVATION

If this question makes you nervous, ask the Lord what your heart needs to know and what truth you need to know. Journal His response here.

Journal what He says to you about how much money you're personally called to steward for the Kingdom of God in your lifetime. Ask Him for strategies for you. Commit to being faithful to His response.

_____
_____
_____
_____
_____
_____
_____
_____
_____

The second question the Lord showed me was while I was watching the 2016 movie, *Sully*. It's the true story of US Airways Pilot Captain Chesley "Sully" Sullenberger's successful emergency landing in New York's Hudson River. The Captain is a true hero and refused to leave the partially submerged aircraft until all 155 passengers and crew from his flight manifest were successfully rescued. In the movie, Captain Sully proclaimed that he was responsible for 155 souls. After he said that, the Holy Spirit said to me, "Ask Me how many souls you're responsible for?" I wept as I heard His question. I'd never considered that before. I'm responsible for a predetermined number of souls on this planet. And so are you. How we're responsible for the souls in our journey can vary. Some have the responsibility for evangelism, others for equipping and mothering and fathering.

PRAYER ACTIVATION

Ask the Lord how many souls you're responsible for in your lifetime and in what ways you're called to serve them. Ask Him for help being faithful with this call on your life. Journal below.

_____
_____
_____
_____
_____
_____
_____
_____
_____
_____
_____

God's Heart

CHAPTER 2

GETTING HEALTHY: SPIRIT, SOUL, & BODY

As children of God, we are triune beings. We are a spirit with a soul comprised of our mind, will and emotions, living in an earthly body. Becoming and remaining healthy in each of these areas is a key component to running our race well. Set your heart to pursue a healthy heart through journeying with God. Scripture has lots to say regarding different areas of health.

3 John 2 perhaps sums up the Lord's heart for His people best, "Beloved, I pray that you may prosper in all things and be in health, just as your soul prospers." This verse gives a key to prosperity: prosperity of soul (mind, will, emotions) will determine the health of our spirits and our bodies.

Our souls have the capacity to get wounded through life trauma in our formative years and beyond. We don't get to choose our families and the level of mental health the members walk in. What we can choose is what we do about learning healthy tools and getting healed once we're grown. You'll experience some dimensions of immediate healing breakthrough and other healings will be a process.

Either way, the best part of life is that God is walking with you in the journey. No matter if things go well or not, the fact that He is with you is your greatest treasure.

I had a dream once where God spoke to me and told me what the biggest predictor for happiness in marriage is. He said it's good character. Two people who are mature and walk in good character have the greatest capacity for marital happiness. He said character as it relates to happiness is more important than even being a Believer. How much more powerful is it then when Believers of strong character are married? One of the Holy Spirit's primary goals in our individual lives is to grow us in maturity and character. Getting healed and growing up emotionally is important in realizing maturity and character.

There are a number of steps we can take to become healthy and grow in character. When we say yes to Jesus, the Holy Spirit takes us on a journey toward relationship with the Trinity and towards health. Hebrews 12:1-2 exhorts us to emulate Jesus, "Therefore we also, since we are surrounded by so great a cloud of witnesses, let us lay aside every weight, and the sin which so easily ensnares us, and let us run with endurance the race that is set before us, looking unto Jesus, the author and finisher of our faith, who for the joy that was set before Him endured the cross, despising the shame, and has sat down at the right hand of the throne of God." Jesus focused on the prize of relationship with us. By doing so, He was able to do the hard things His life entailed. When we have the same focus of loving God and loving people, we can also do hard things. There are lots of things in life that aren't fun: changing dirty diapers, being up at night with a child, chores, college work, working late, and many other things. If we focused on the things we don't enjoy, we wouldn't persevere to accomplish the tasks God gives us. Focusing on the big picture grows us into maturity and allows us to do all things with integrity.

Sin

Hebrews Chapter 12 goes on to reveal that Father God disciplines us like a Father so that we may be "partakers of His holiness" and even though it is painful, "afterward it yields the peaceable fruit of righteousness to those who have been trained by it". It's important that we surrender to the Cross and stop sinning. God promises that no longer sinning is possible with His help. 1 Corinthians 10:13 tells us, "No temptation has overtaken you except such as is common to man; but God is faithful, who will not allow you to be tempted beyond what you are able, but with the temptation will also make the way of escape, that you may be able to bear it."

Sin in our lives and in our generational lines opens the doors to demonic oppression. A sign that the demonic is involved in a person's emotions or thoughts is that the temptation toward sinful behavior is so strong it nearly compels the person to sin. Therefore, it is critical that the person press into God for the way of escape because Scripture describes the battle with, "For the weapons of our warfare are not carnal but mighty in God for pulling down strongholds, casting down arguments and every high thing that exalts itself against the knowledge of God, bringing every thought into captivity to the obedience of Christ." 2 Corinthians 10:4-5. This verse describes the spiritual battle we face in our thoughts and emotions that the enemy plants to get us to sin and therefore into demonic oppression. When we take every thought and every emotion captive, to the obedience of Christ, we're able to live victorious lives. Eventually, the temptation for a particular sin will cease as the person walks in freedom. A person will not be perpetually tormented by temptation and previous sin. In John 10:10 Jesus describes the lives we lead, "The thief does not come except to steal, and to kill, and to destroy. I have come that they may have life, and that they may have it more abundantly." As we press into relationship with Jesus, He heals our wounds and brings more abundant life.

When we understand the call on our lives and living for eternity, sin won't be attractive because we don't want to hurt our Father's heart and diminish what Jesus' death on the Cross paid for. We also won't want to experience the time that healing takes away from building for eternity. 2 Corinthians 7:1 sums this concept up well, "Therefore, having these promises, beloved, let us cleanse ourselves from all filthiness of the flesh and spirit, perfecting holiness in the fear of God." Philippians 2:12-13 exhorts us as light bearers to, "Therefore, my beloved, as you have always obeyed, not as in my presence only, but now much more in my absence, work out your own salvation with fear and trembling; for it is God who works in you both to will and to do for His good pleasure."

PRAYER ACTIVATION

Take some time now and repent for any active sin in your life. Ask the Lord to heal your heart and bring you into deeper relationship with Him. Journal what you sense Him saying to your heart.

_____
_____
_____
_____
_____
_____
_____
_____

Pain and Pressure

The level of joy, peace and love that we live in on a daily basis is a litmus test for the reality of our heart knowing that we're deeply loved by God. Experiencing routine emotions of fear and anxiety is a sign that we don't really know that God loves us, protects us, and provides for us. If peace and joy are not your daily emotional heart stance, pursue a deeper relationship with God and heart healing tools. Please understand that this is a process and a journey that God invites us to undertake.

My process for living life peacefully and joyfully unfolded over many years. I felt fearful and anxious on a daily basis. I began to get many prophetic words about how peaceful of a person I was and how my atmosphere of peace permeated and changed people around me. The first few times I received this word, my husband commented that the words must be wrong because we both knew I was anything but peaceful. In reality, the prophetic words began a journey with the Lord where He brought heart healing and a revelation of His love for me that built my spirit into a place of peace. Then I began to receive words of how joyful I was. When my husband laughed at those words, I reminded him of the peace process and we both understood that God was bringing me into becoming joyful. One night while I was sleeping, the presence of God filled my room so completely that I awoke. I realized that for the first time in my life I didn't feel an ounce of fear. In Him is complete peace and fullness of joy. Then He spoke Romans 14:17 to me, "for the kingdom of God is not eating and drinking, but righteousness and peace and joy in the Holy Spirit." When He said that, I understood He had taken me on a journey through first deeply understanding my complete acceptance and righteousness in Christ, then in building peace into me, and finally, onto a season of joy.

PRAYER ACTIVATION

Where are you currently in this process? Do you routinely experience peace and joy? Or are anxiety and fear still common emotions? If that's a difficult question to answer or the question itself evokes fear, ask the Lord what your heart needs to know. Journal below.

_____
_____
_____
_____
_____
_____
_____
_____
_____
_____
_____
_____
_____
_____
_____

While understanding our current level of heart emotional health, we need to realize that everyone experiences circumstantial pain and pressure in life. The key is being strategic with what tools we choose to use to deal with the pain and pressure. There are plenty of unhealthy tools that will bring more pain and brokenness such as alcohol, drugs, pornography, overeating, shopping, gambling, grumbling, sex outside of marriage, excessive video gaming and other avoidance behaviors. Healthy tools will not only bring a solution to whatever is causing the pain and pressure, but will bring life to the person. Tools such as exercising, praying, soaking, talking with friends and family, worshiping, praying in tongues, working, and cleaning can all help bring clarity.

PRAYER ACTIVATION

Identify and journal what unhealthy tools you currently use when you experience pain and pressure. Ask the Lord for help in getting free from unhealthy tools and ask Him what healthy tools you can develop instead.

_____
_____
_____
_____
_____
_____
_____
_____
_____
_____
_____
_____
_____
_____
_____

Forgiveness

Scripture commands us to forgive others just as God forgave us of our sins when we repented. Matthew 6:14-15 exhorts us, "For if you forgive other people when they sin against you, your heavenly Father will also forgive you. But if you do not forgive others their sins, your Father will not forgive your sins." This is such a powerful testament to the nature of forgiveness. We forgive others because our Father first forgave us. We're not allowed to withhold forgiveness from others. If we have unforgiveness, it allows the enemy legal access to us to torment us and bring evil into our lives. Unforgiveness leads to bitter root judgments that fester in our own hearts bringing destruction. John Arnott wrote a powerful in depth book called "Forgiveness" on this topic. Many people experience healing and miracles when they release people from their judgments. It's important that we live a lifestyle of forgiveness. Forgiveness is often not a "one and done" thing. It's often a process for our heart to heal. As we choose to forgive, our emotions will (eventually) line up with our choice to bless. Choosing to forgive someone does not mean that what they did is acceptable or condoned. We still need to have healthy boundaries with people. Forgiving them does not mean that they deserve our trust or have unlimited access to our lives. Psalms 4:26 exhorts us to, "Be angry, and do not sin." Sin comes in when we become offended or harbor unforgiveness and bitterness. Offense and unforgiveness are major hooks that the enemy uses to bring God's people into bondage and to usurp their power and authority in the world. We would be wise to be hyper vigilant to not take offense, not become jealous and to keep short accounts with people.

A short powerful prayer to help keep your heart healthy and in check is "Lord, I forgive (name of person). I release (name) from my judgments. I bless him/her and ask You to bless him/her." Pray this as often as you feel offended or jealous. Your heart will line up with what God is doing if you pursue forgiveness.

Needing to forgive people to keep our hearts pure to walk in love is not a new phenomenon. God instructs us in Colossians 3:12-17, "Therefore, as the elect of God, holy and beloved, put on tender mercies, kindness, humility, meekness, longsuffering; bearing with one another, and forgiving one another, if anyone has a complaint against another; even as Christ forgave you, so you also must do. But above all these things put on love, which is the bond of perfection. And let the peace of God rule in your hearts, to which also you were called in one body; and be thankful. Let the word of Christ dwell in you richly in all wisdom, teaching and admonishing one another in psalms and hymns and spiritual songs, singing with grace in your hearts to the Lord. And whatever you do in word or deed, do all in the name of the Lord Jesus, giving thanks to God the Father through Him."

PRAYER ACTIVATION

Take a few minutes now and ask Holy Spirit if you need to repent for taking offense and if there is anyone you need to forgive. Ask Him to remove any veils of deception from your eyes and heart. Journal any strategies the Lord gives you here for remaining free from offense and any boundaries you need to set with people in your life.

_____
_____
_____
_____
_____

Soul Ties

Soul ties are links in the spirit that connect two people to each other. Soul ties can be beneficial or detrimental, depending upon the situation. The Bible talks about David and Jonathan's covenant with each other in 1 Samuel 18:1-3, "Now when he had finished speaking to Saul, the soul of Jonathan was knit to the soul of David, and Jonathan loved him as his own soul. Saul took him that day, and would not let him go home to his father's house anymore. Then Jonathan and David made a covenant, because he loved him as his own soul." This was a pure relationship and they became covenant family to each other in friendship.

Husbands and wives form soul ties with one another when they marry. The soul tie helps keep their hearts connected to one another. When families are emotionally healthy, the members form soul ties that help maintain relationships and bond the members together.

Unhealthy soul ties can be devastating to a person's emotional health because it can fracture the person's soul. Soul ties are unhealthy when a relationship is unhealthy and has components of abuse. In those instances, the soul tie serves to keep the members bound together in an unhealthy system. Unhealthy soul ties between parents and adult children can keep the children from bonding with their own spouses. If that exists, the soul ties between the parents and adult children need to be broken in the spirit. Genesis 2:24 explains the new bond that must be formed for a healthy marriage to exist, "Therefore a man shall leave his father and mother and be joined to his wife, and they shall become one flesh." The new marriage must be the primary relationship for the adult child, not the parent/child relationship.

    Unhealthy soul ties can be formed before marriage (or during marriage if there is infidelity) with sexual activity, lust, or fantasy emotional connection. Viewing pornography forms soul ties between the viewer and viewed. Also, reading romance novels or viewing romantic movies and fantasizing about emotional connection with the people can form soul ties. This tends to happen more for women than men, even if there isn't sexual fantasy involved. The formation of soul ties for young people in dating relationships is what can be so detrimental for them in prohibiting bonding with their future spouse. The female can form a soul tie just through emotional connection even if there isn't sexual activity. There are hormones released in the brain that are for the God given purpose of bonding people together. Oxytocin is one of those hormones. It's an extremely powerful bonding agent. It's released when a mother breastfeeds her child and it works to bond the mother and the baby. Oxytocin is also released when a man ejaculates. God designed the release of oxytocin to bond the man to his wife during sexual intimacy. The problem comes in when he releases oxytocin through pornography and becomes bonded in the spirit to whatever he was viewing. We are designed to bond with one spouse for a lifetime. When we have released oxytocin repeatedly prior to marriage either through multiple dating relationships or sexual encounters, our ability to bond successfully to our future spouse decreases. As parents, because of the power of soul ties and oxytocin as bonding agents it is wise to encourage our children to wait to date or limit dating until they're ready to marry.

Mercifully, God is the God of redemption. He provides supernatural healing for those who have become fractured and are limited in their ability to bond.

Prayer to Break Unhealthy Soul Ties

Fortunately, unhealthy soul ties are easy to break.

"I break a soul tie with (name of person). I send back to him/her what is his/hers covered in the Blood of Jesus and I take back what's mine covered in the Blood of Jesus." Then clap once.

Repeat for each person a soul tie exists with outside of marriage. If you're not sure if your soul tie with your parents is healthy, you can break any unhealthy aspect of it and leave the healthy part intact by saying, "I break any unhealthy soul ties with (name of person)." And continue the remainder of the prayer above. If you've viewed pornography or fantasized about people emotionally but you don't know their names, you can break the soul ties by saying, "I break soul ties with all people I've sexually/emotionally fantasized about." And continue with the remainder of the prayer above.

Take some time with the Lord now and break unhealthy soul ties. Break the soul ties with everyone He highlights to you. Ask Him to restore your purity to you and heal your heart. Rest in His Presence and His goodness as He refreshes your soul. You should feel lighter once you've completed this.

I pray for His healing for you, for your soul, and for your heart. I pray that you'd successfully be able to bond to your spouse and your family in healthy ways. I also pray that God would heal the neuro pathways in your brain and create new ones for healthy relationships.

Healed from Co-dependency, Addictions and Other Unhealthy Soul Patterns

The family dynamics and systems we grow up in form our experiences and expectations for what relationships and communication entail. If we grow up with unhealthy parents, codependency and addictions are often our own go to patterns unless we take active steps to change how we see and communicate. People tend to marry people who are at the same emotional level of health that they are. If it's an unhealthy level, marital patterns will develop that contribute to further codependency and addiction. Codependency is defined as "excessive emotional or psychological reliance on a partner, typically a partner who requires support due to an illness or addiction." Codependent relationships are extremely destructive to everyone involved in the family system. The good news is, if you learned an unhealthy system growing up, you can learn a healthy system now that you're grown. It is worth it to yourself, your children and your future generations to get your soul healed and develop healthy communication patterns. There are lots of resources available for people who want to grow and change. Melody Beatty wrote the famous codependency series. Her latest is "Healed from Codependency". Brene Brown has studied and written extensively on shame, empathy, courage and vulnerability and carries an anointing for healing the soul. AA has classes in most cities that help people get healed from codependency and addictions. Catch the Fire hosts a number of classes throughout the year that teach life skills and bring healing, including *Love After Marriage* classes, *Single Life* classes, *Reforming* classes which helps people who did not grow up with healthy skills, *Loving Your Kids on Purpose* for healthy parenting skills, *Thrive* for becoming healthy and mature. In addition, there are ministries available that provide heart healing and deliverance through *Heart Sync Ministry*, *Sozo Ministry*, *RTF* (Restoring the Foundations), and *Ignite* groups for people to experience community together. People learn through experience. Catch the Fire carries an anointing to do family and community well. Psalms 68:5-6 shows the compassion of our Father, "A father of the fatherless, a defender of widows, Is God in His holy habitation. God sets the solitary in families; He brings out those who are bound into prosperity; but the rebellious dwell in a dry land." Ask God to put you in a family to learn to apply healthy tools and skills.

Be very careful with allowing pop culture to define relationships and identity for you. The book "50 Shades of Grey" is needless to say not a healthy model for sexuality. Many celebrities' view of the world should not define yours. Be careful with your eye gates and ear gates about what you're allowing in because, "As a man thinks in his heart, so is he." Proverbs 23:7.

PRAYER ACTIVATION

Ask the Lord if there is anything you need to lay aside in order for you to become healthy. (Relationships? Habits? Patterns? Media? Music?) Write what He shows you here and commit to obey.

_____
_____
_____
_____
_____

Healthy people have an ongoing lifestyle of healing and stewarding their hearts. We're all in process and on a journey. When something happens that you have a reaction to, use the opportunity to pursue healing and truth. Ask God what your heart needs to know. Identify ungodly beliefs and where your thoughts aren't congruent with what Scripture teaches. Reading the Bible regularly helps renew your mind with truth. Rewire your brain and your thoughts through Scripture. Take responsibility to get healthy emotionally. Give yourself grace but keep moving forward.

PRAYER ACTIVATION

Dialogue with God about what steps you need to take to incorporate health into your soul. Journal here.

Generational Legacy

It is our honor to be chosen by God and to be people who run our races well and who live for legacy; people who steward revival well and pass it on to the next generation. Throughout history, revival has always ended. There has heretofore not been a generation who has carried God's revival forward through the generations. We have the opportunity to be the first. In order to do so, we have to live our lives pursuing God, stewarding His call on our lives for a generation we may not see. We don't want to be like King Hezekiah in the Bible who lived only for himself at the expense of his future generations. He was an Israeli king who begged for mercy and extended life for himself but his children and grandchildren paid the price for it.

2 Kings 20:1-21 tells the story, 'In those days Hezekiah was sick and near death. And Isaiah the prophet, the son of Amoz, went to him and said to him, 'Thus says the Lord: 'Set your house in order, for you shall die, and not live.'" Then he turned his face toward the wall, and prayed to the Lord, saying, "Remember now, O Lord, I pray, how I have walked before You in truth with a loyal heart, and have done what was good in Your sight." And Hezekiah wept bitterly. And it happened, before Isaiah had gone out into the middle court, that the word of the Lord came to him, saying, "Return and tell Hezekiah the leader of My people, 'Thus says the Lord, the

God of David your father: "I have heard your prayer, I have seen your tears; surely I will heal you. On the third day you shall go up to the house of the Lord. And I will add to your days fifteen years. I will deliver you and this city from the hand of the king of Assyria; and I will defend this city for My own sake, and for the sake of My servant David.""" Then Isaiah said, "Take a lump of figs." So they took and laid it on the boil, and he recovered. And Hezekiah said to Isaiah, "What is the sign that the Lord will heal me, and that I shall go up to the house of the Lord the third day?" Then Isaiah said, "This is the sign to you from the Lord, that the Lord will do the thing which He has spoken: shall the shadow go forward ten degrees or go backward ten degrees?" And Hezekiah answered, "It is an easy thing for the shadow to go down ten degrees; no, but let the shadow go backward ten degrees." So Isaiah the prophet cried out to the Lord, and He brought the shadow ten degrees backward, by which it had gone down on the sundial of Ahaz. At that time Berodach-Baladan the son of Baladan, king of Babylon, sent letters and a present to Hezekiah, for he heard that Hezekiah had been sick. And Hezekiah was attentive to them, and showed them all the house of his treasures- the silver and gold, the spices and precious ointment, and all his armory- all that was found among his treasures. There was nothing in his house or in all his dominion that Hezekiah did not show them. Then Isaiah the prophet went to King Hezekiah, and said to him, "What did these men say, and from where did they come to you?" So Hezekiah said, "They came from a far country, from Babylon." And he said, "What have they seen in your house?" So Hezekiah answered, "They have seen all that is in my house; there is nothing among my treasures that I have not shown them." Then Isaiah said to Hezekiah, "Hear the word of the Lord: 'Behold, the days are coming when all that is in your house, and what your fathers have accumulated until this day, shall be carried to Babylon; nothing shall be left,' says the Lord. 'And they shall take away some of your sons who will descend from you, whom you will beget; and they shall be eunuchs in the palace of the king of Babylon.'" So Hezekiah said to Isaiah, "The word of the Lord which you have spoken is good!" For he said, "Will there not be peace and truth at least in my days?"'

We have the opportunity to be the generation who lives for legacy and doesn't pass iniquity or problems onto the next generation. In my personal life, God moved our family to Redding, California for an 8-year season. Things became very challenging for us financially while we were there. As the financial problems began, I began to plan for our family to move to Texas. I was only fifteen seconds into planning our escape when the Lord shouted, "JONAH!" to me. He was so loud, I sat back stunned. He went on to say to me, "I'm in this season here in Redding for you, Annie. Don't run." Hearing His voice, I agreed to stay. The season devastated us financially. Towards the end of our years in Redding, I had a dream. In the dream, Pastor Bill Johnson prayed for our financial restoration and told me that our radical obedience to the Lord, even through the pain, had a tremendous effect on our generational line. He said we took down five demonic giants against our family line through our obedience and that we and our children would walk in freedom in those areas now. When I awoke, I could feel the pleasure of my Father over me.

Are we willing to do hard and painful things for a generation we may never see? If so, God's kingdom will be extended over the earth and we will be richly rewarded in Heaven for our devotion to Jesus.

PRAYER ACTIVATION

Listen to God and journal what He shows you. Lay aside any compromise in your life. Commit to live for legacy. Write any practical steps He's asking you to take.

_____

_____

Spirit Health

Healthy spirits result from deep relationship with God and from obtaining necessary inner healing, individual deliverance and generational repentance and deliverance. Unconfessed sin from generational lines allows the enemy legal access to bring torment and destruction to a person. Fortunately, identificational repentance and confession of sin on behalf of our family lines can bring about the freedom and the generational blessings that Jesus paid for through His death and resurrection. I've found two effective routes to bring a lot of freedom. The first is a book of generational repentance prayers called "Silencing the Accuser" by Jacquelin and Daniel Hanselman. I strongly recommend you purchase the book and pray aloud the prayers. Great freedom will likely ensue. The other prayer I recommend every Believer pray aloud is repentance from freemasonry. Freemasonry was so widespread throughout the Americas, Europe, and other regions that nearly everyone has it somewhere in their generational line, most often without awareness of an ancestor or family member's involvement. Many prayers for repentance from freemasonry can be found online. I particularly like one from Jubilee Resources (www.jubileeresources.org). I also recommend that you pray it aloud with another person present to intercede on your behalf or pray it aloud together with another person. In deliverance circles, I've heard it mentioned that the freemasons embedded a reverse curse of poverty to come upon a person in the event that they or their family left freemasonry. After praying through the freemasonry prayer of release, simply break the reverse curse of poverty off of you and your family. That can be done by saying, "I break the reverse curse of poverty off of me and my family line from freemasonry now in Jesus name. Thank you, Lord, for life and life more abundantly and financial prosperity."

Understand that freedom can be a process. As you continue to walk in relationship with God, He'll highlight areas that you need freedom and healing in and how to receive it.

Our spirits need interaction with God through praise, worship, prayer, praying in tongues, soaking prayer, reading the Word of God, listening to Him, doing the will of God, and other ways. Just like our bodies need food and sleep to be healthy, our spirits need God encounters to be fed. The following Scriptures highlight Jesus being our spiritual food.

Jesus told His disciples about spiritual food in John 4:31-34, "In the meantime His disciples urged Him, saying, "Rabbi, eat." But He said to them, "I have food to eat of which you do not know." Therefore, the disciples said to one another, "Has anyone brought Him anything to eat?" Jesus said to them, "My food is to do the will of Him who sent Me, and to finish His work.""

Jesus promised us that He would provide for our spiritual thirst in John 7:37-38, "On the last day, that great day of the feast, Jesus stood and cried out, saying, "If anyone thirsts, let him come to Me and drink. He who believes in Me, as the Scripture has said, out of his heart will flow rivers of living water."

And another promise is found in John 6:32-3, "Then Jesus said to them, "Most assuredly, I say to you, Moses did not give you the bread from heaven, but My Father gives you the true bread from heaven. For the bread of God is He who comes down from heaven and gives life to the world." Then they said to Him, "Lord, give us this bread always." And Jesus said to them, "I am the bread of life. He who comes to Me shall never hunger, and he who believes in Me shall never thirst.""

In Matthew 4:3-4, when satan was tempting Jesus in the wilderness to turn stones into bread to satiate his hunger, Jesus responded with, "But He answered and said, "It is written, 'Man shall not live by bread alone, but by every word that proceeds from the mouth of God.'"

If Jesus, who was fully God and fully man, needed the spiritual food of communing with His Father in prayer and reading the Word of God while He walked the earth, how much more do we need to follow His example to be healthy in our spirits?

Another important need for our spirit is to know who God is, to know who we are and to know what we were created to do. The prophetic answers all three of those questions and as we pursue God, He'll show us the answers to the deep cry of our hearts.

Jesus paid for our full freedom that we would walk as the manifest sons of God on this earth, bringing Heaven to earth. Just because He paid for it on the Cross doesn't mean that individuals fully have that freedom. Matthew 11:12 explains this concept, "And from the days of John the Baptist until now the kingdom of heaven suffers violence, and the violent take it by force." Our freedom has been paid for but it's up to us to appropriate it for ourselves and our families. If this were not true, the minute you received Christ as your Savior, you would be completely healed, delivered and free in all areas of your life. Since this is obviously not true through observation, we understand that we have a role to play in receiving all that Jesus paid for.

PRAYER ACTIVATION

Journal here and ask God what steps you need to take now to more fully appropriate Christ's freedom in your life.

_____
_____
_____
_____
_____
_____
_____
_____
_____
_____
_____
_____
_____
_____

Body Health

In order to fully run our races well and accomplish the call on our lives, we must have healthy bodies for the journey. Proper sleep, nutrition, exercise, water, vitamins, maintaining a healthy weight and other tools are key to a healthy physical lifestyle. Any of these areas that you're not currently in balance in, ask God for any truth you need to know and any strategies to bring your body into divine health. Isaiah 53:4-5 prophesied what Jesus would pay for with His death for us regarding health, "Surely He has borne our griefs and carried our sorrows; Yet we esteemed Him stricken, smitten by God, and afflicted. But He was wounded for our transgressions, He was bruised for our iniquities; the chastisement for our peace was upon Him, and by His stripes we are healed."

God foresaw every imaginable sin and healing that we would need and intentionally paid for it over two thousand years ago. We receive our healing through faith that Jesus already accomplished it for us on the Cross. Sometimes, it's simple to receive a healing and sometimes it takes more effort on our part, but either way, it's already been paid for and is available to us. We have a responsibility to care for our bodies naturally and pursue any healing naturally and spiritually that we need. Romans 12:1-2 exhorts us to serve with our lives, "I beseech you therefore, brethren, by the mercies of God, that you present your bodies a living sacrifice, holy, acceptable to God, which is your reasonable service. And do not be conformed to this world, but be transformed by the renewing of your mind, that you may prove what is that good and acceptable and perfect will of God."

Rest is a weapon. Getting enough rest for our bodies and our souls is important for us to live well. Often, when we're feeling stressed out, taking a nap or getting more sleep will give us the capacity to face our problems. Life comes in waves. Pain and problems come in waves. If we understand that seasons eventually change, as long as we're pursuing health and aren't stuck in poverty and lack cycles, the steps we're taking to move forward will help us prosper. Just like contractions in the birthing process, if we can ride out the wave, we can take steps to thrive in the rest cycles. Learning to live in the rest of God by knowing that we're deeply loved helps us to overcome any challenge and thrive in life. This rest comes through meditating on His word, through soaking in His presence, through worship, through journaling, through daily walking with Him. When the Lord calls us into relationship and specifically into wilderness seasons in our lives, it's to draw us closer to Him. Walking in sonship, experiencing the love of the Father produces a deep rest in our souls. My ultimate revelation through our Redding wilderness season was that the greatest treasure in life is being with God. Circumstances going well or not going well don't matter. The real prize in life is relationship with Him. That revelation brings a deep rest.

PRAYER ACTIVATION

Is your soul currently able to abide with God in rest? Take some time to talk with God regarding this rest and what steps you can take. Also, ask Him what your heart needs to know to enter rest. I pray for you, that you'll enter the rest of God and walk closely with Him in life. Journal below.

_____
_____
_____
_____
_____
_____

Regularly celebrating Communion with the elements of Jesus' body and blood both at church and at home, can bring healing to our bodies, our souls, and our spirits. Meditating on Jesus' love and sacrifice for us is important. The Blood of Jesus is powerful. He paid the ultimate price to redeem us. Scientists have determined that there are 39 root causes of disease. Jesus took 39 lashes. Coincidence? No. God provided payment for every possible ailment. Jesus suffered with a crown of thorns on His head. That paid for us to have peace and a sound mind. Jesus died so that we may have life and life more abundantly (John 10:10). Celebrating Communion puts us in remembrance of His sacrifice and builds our faith for healing. My brother's knees were healed years ago as he took Communion at church. The healing enabled him to follow the call on his life to join the Army and become a Kiowa helicopter pilot.

Pastor Jim Banks of House of Healing Ministries has been helping bring physical and emotional healing from trauma for over a decade. He has a 23-minute prayer that you can stream online to help bring healing to your physical body. He suggests you lay down while he prays over you in the recording. It's a very healing experience. That prayer can be found online at www.houseofhealingministries.org.

PRAYER ACTIVATION

Journal here any physical areas that you need to bring into health. Ask God what He has to say to help you.

_____
_____
_____
_____
_____
_____
_____
_____
_____
_____
_____
_____

Living with Margin

Margin is defined as "the edge or border of something" or "an amount by which a thing is won or falls short". The greater a margin, the less risk exists. People who live without margin financially live paycheck to paycheck. Any hiccup or interruption in a paycheck can cause catastrophic issues for them financially. People who live without margin or live with very little margin health wise can become very ill if they don't get enough sleep one night or skip a meal. People who live without margin in their soul or their spirit can become easily offended or depressed if something untoward happens. As people of God, we're called to live healthy lives spirit, soul, and body. We need to intentionally build in margin so that we can weather the storms of life and bring the Kingdom of God to earth. Jesus modeled building in margin by fasting and praying before He needed the withdrawal of spiritual power for a healing. In Matthew 17:14-21 Jesus explains the importance of prayer and fasting, "And when they had come to the multitude, a man came to Him, kneeling down to Him and saying, "Lord, have mercy on my son, for he is an epileptic and suffers severely; for he often falls into the fire and often into the water. So I brought him to Your disciples, but they could not cure him." Then Jesus answered and said, "O faithless and perverse generation, how long shall I be with you? How long shall I bear with you? Bring him here to Me." And Jesus rebuked the demon, and it came out of him; and the child was cured from that very hour. Then the disciples came to Jesus privately and said, "Why could we not cast it out?" So Jesus said to them, "Because of your unbelief; for assuredly, I say to you, if you have faith as a mustard seed, you will say to this mountain, 'Move from here to there.' And it will move; and nothing will be impossible for you. However, this kind does not go out except by prayer and fasting." Jesus neither fasted nor prayed right then to be able to bring deliverance to the boy. He had the power stored up for the occasion through previous prayer and fasting. Jesus lived with a large margin in all areas of His life and is a model for how we should live.

PRAYER ACTIVATION

Journal and ask God what areas of your life need greater margin and what to do to build in margin in your life.

_____
_____
_____
_____
_____
_____
_____
_____
_____
_____
_____
_____

God's Heart

CHAPTER 3

GETTING EQUIPPED & COMPETENT

We each need to develop a tool belt full of tools to do life in the spirit well and to help us grow up into maturity. The overall big picture of our lives is that God loves us beyond measure and that He has a purpose for us to accomplish here on earth. When we walk out our lives with both the truth of His love for us and the fear of the Lord, we'll live life well. The fear of the Lord is discussed throughout Scripture. It does not mean that we need to be afraid of God. After all, He is a good Father. What it does mean is that He is worthy of awe and respect. Proverbs 1:7 says, "The fear of the Lord is the beginning of knowledge, but fools despise wisdom and instruction." Knowing that God loves you helps you manage your behavior well because you want to protect the intimacy you have with God. Knowing that one day you'll stand before God to give an account of your life helps you make good choices day to day. Anything that stands in the way of your ability to live well and make good choices can mean that you need some inner healing, or deliverance, or renewing of your mind, or inner resolve to stop sinning and making bad choices. If you find that you're struggling, pursue deeper relationship with God and pursue heart healing. Human beings are complicated and intricately made. God is in the business of restoring His people and walks with us every step of the way. Pursue getting healed and getting equipped and help other people do the same.

When my husband and I were first married, I was getting healed from growing up in an alcoholic/codependent home. My husband grew up in a healthy home and while he had a lot of grace for my learning curve, we knew I was not an equal marriage partner for him because of my brokenness. One anniversary weekend early in our marriage, Joe encouraged me to continue pursuing healing. I told him I was tired and wanted to rest for a while. He responded by saying that I was still pretty broken and couldn't afford to stop there and had to move forward quickly. I knew he was right and knew that if I was going to be a good marriage partner to him, I had to keep moving as quickly as possible. If you're currently in a broken place, I encourage you to pursue healing and not stop. Your future relationships will thank you for it. A few years later once we'd started having children, I was very thankful for all the work I'd already done.

Also, no matter what level of healthy family you grew up in, once you become an adult at eighteen years old, you and God can go on a journey towards health. You don't have to stay broken. You can take responsibility for your life and grow into a healthy, mature adult. Like I did, you may have a lot of healing to do. Be confident that God will walk the process with you. He'll never leave you nor forsake you.

Practical steps to take for healing from codependency include reading the *Codependent No More* book series by Melody Beattie; reading Danny Silk's book on *Loving Your Kids on Purpose*, taking the relationship classes offered at Catch the Fire, and anything else the Lord highlights to you. Even if you don't yet have kids, Danny Silk's book is great for learning to do relationships well.

It took nearly a decade for my soul to get healed and for me to develop healthy communication patterns and to no longer be codependent. When that process was done, God began opening up realms of the spirit to me and started showing us what the call on our lives were. I know that had I not worked diligently to get healthy, I would not have gotten to the point of knowing about my call or knowing the Lord in a deeper way. The call would have passed on to the next generation. My process was unique to me. Other people develop in the spirit before they heal in the soul. Whatever your process is, be faithful to run your race well.

I remember hearing Worship leader Brian Johnson, from Bethel, preach once about being faithful to run your race well. He said if he were not aware of standing before God someday to give an account of his life he would have chosen to use his musical ability to become a country singer and sit in his hot tub with his beautiful wife and relax in his success. Instead, he knows he personally has a call on his life to lead people into worship in the church and equip people to bring the Kingdom. Whether you're called to build a business for God, raise children, be an accountant, be an actress or a rock star, be a car mechanic, or some other profession, do it with all of your heart to bring Jesus glory.

PRAYER ACTIVATION

Take some time here to search your heart and journal below. If you're not currently on track to live your life well, repent and make the necessary adjustments. Ask God to show you where you are and what your next steps need to be. If you're on track, write your next steps here. If this brought up any fear for you, ask God for His perfect love. 1 John 4:17-19 says, "Love has been perfected among us in this: that we may have boldness in the day of judgment; because as He is, so are we in this world. There is no fear in love; but perfect love casts out fear, because fear involves torment. But he who fears has not been made perfect in love. We love Him because He first loved us."

Annie Blouin

What these verses say to us is that if we're walking in relationship with God, He'll direct our steps and we can rest in His perfect love and be confident in standing before Him to account for our lives. 2 Corinthians 3:4-6 says, "And we have such trust through Christ toward God. Not that we are sufficient of ourselves to think of anything as being from ourselves, but our sufficiency is from God, who also made us sufficient as ministers of the new covenant, not of the letter but of the Spirit; for the letter kills, but the Spirit gives life."

If you feel afraid that you're behind the Lord's schedule for your life and that you should have accomplished more by this point, I want to encourage you that the Lord factored in the potential brokenness, the enemy attacks, your own mistakes and other things into your life call. You're not a machine and the Lord doesn't expect you to be. The Lord also has the ability to accelerate you into destiny to catch you up if you did fall behind.

I had a dream of a gyroscope type instrument in July of 2014 in Redding. As I watched it spin in multiple directions, the Lord said to pray that I lined up with His time and space continuum. I saw that in the spirit the gyroscope needed to be perfectly aligned for the next step of my life. When I woke up, the Lord showed me that when an aircraft flies across country, pointing it in the general direction of it's destination and making slight adjustments along the way for wind and weather considerations is sufficient until it's approaching the final landing. Then the exact coordinates need to be achieved for the plane to land safely on the runway. We were at the landing place in our lives and needed to line up with His time and space continuum. I prayed that we'd line up and frankly didn't have full understanding of what that meant. Two months later in September 2014, the Lord moved us to Catch the Fire in Raleigh/Durham, North Carolina and we're so thankful He did.

He told me the Body of Christ was going through a door into destiny in October 2017 and told me to pray that we'd all line up with His time and space continuum again. As of this writing, it's too early to tell what that means for individuals, but I know it's significant based on our prior experience.

PRAYER ACTIVATION

Take a moment and ask God if you're in line with His plan for your life timing wise. If He says no, ask Him to accelerate you and pray that you'd line up with His time and space continuum and watch what He does in your life. Make any notes here so that you'll remember what God said to you.

_____
_____
_____
_____
_____
_____
_____
_____
_____
_____
_____
_____
_____
_____

The Lord wants us to grow up into maturity in our lives and in the things of God. The writer of Hebrews exhorts us to become mature spiritually in 5:12-14, "For though by this time you ought to be teachers, you need someone to teach you again the first principles of the oracles of God; and you have come to need milk and not solid food. For everyone who partakes only of milk is unskilled in the word of righteousness, for he is a babe. But solid food belongs to those who are of full age, that those who by reason of use have their senses exercised to discern both good and evil." Being diligent to study the Word, and apply the principles of God with the Holy Spirit will help you to grow into maturity.

In a dream I had twelve years ago, a friend asked me the secret to parenting. I confidently told her "training". When I awoke, I knew God had just given me wisdom. Our job as parents is to train our children in the practical things of life, in character, in loving God well, in making good choices and many other things. If we teach and train them well, we do very little disciplining or correcting. They've never done life before and it's our opportunity to raise them well. God treats us the same way. He loves teaching us to do life and helping us build skills. As God's children, it's our pleasure to pursue learning to be competent in the things of the soul, spirit, and body.

Reading the Word, learning to prophesy, praying for healing for the sick, learning to walk in our authority and power as Believers, understanding our authority over destructive weather patterns, ministering deliverance, and many other things are a privilege to train in in our Christian walk.

Expect God to train you in fasting. Fasting is a necessary tool for Christians. Fasting accomplishes many things for us, including: adding power to our prayer, developing character, helping us believe, growing our faith, helping us crucify our carnal nature, giving us deliverance power and other things. If Jesus had to fast while He was on earth, we certainly need to fast.

Luke 4:1-2: "Then Jesus, being filled with the Holy Spirit, returned from the Jordan and was led by the Spirit into the wilderness, being tempted for forty days by the devil. And in those days He ate nothing, and afterward, when they had ended, He was hungry." Luke 4:13-14 tells us the result, "Now when the devil had ended every temptation, he departed from Him until an opportune time. Then Jesus returned in the power of the Spirit to Galilee, and news of Him went out through all the surrounding region."

In May 2007, shortly after a word from Kris Vallotton about God preparing us through a wilderness season and then bringing us into a broad place where we'd bring the Kingdom, the Holy Spirit led us into a wilderness/preparation season. He led us to join a 40 day fast that Lou Engle had called that corresponded with "The Call" in Nashville, Tennessee on July 7, 2007. We did a 40 day Daniel fast where we ate only fruits and vegetables. In the Bible, Daniel thrived and glowed as he only ate fruits and vegetables. I did the opposite. I lost a lot of hair, had little energy and felt horrible. On day 18, I told God that I couldn't take it any longer and that I wanted to quit. His response was firm. He told me that it was necessary for my life's journey that I not cheat and that I complete this fast. I held onto His exhortation and His belief in my ability and I completed the fast. Looking back, I can see the belief, the strength, and the faith that God developed in us through that season. I'm still not a fan of fasting, but I know how important a tool it is and when God prompts a fast, I do it. As a family, God leads us to fast before He transitions us. We fasted before we moved to North Carolina, we fasted before we bought a house, and we fasted before a job promotion for my husband. Fasting provides the fuel and the power for successful upgrades.

The Baptism of the Holy Spirit and making Jesus the Lord of your life, as well as your Savior are both keys to upgrading your walk with God. Acts 2:1-4 tells us of the initial infilling of the Believers with the Holy Spirit, "When the Day of Pentecost had fully come, they were all with one accord in one place. And suddenly there came a sound from heaven, as of a rushing mighty wind, and it filled the whole house where they were sitting. Then there appeared to them divided tongues, as of fire, and one sat upon each of them. And they were all filled with the Holy Spirit and began to speak with other tongues, as the Spirit gave them utterance." The immediate fruit from this Baptism was that the disciples were filled with power and boldness and as they preached three thousand received salvation. This filling of the Holy Spirit is necessary for us today. It creates for us boldness, power, and hunger for God and seeing His kingdom come. It also really helps us to walk in the Gifts of the Holy Spirit.

PRAYER ACTIVATION

If you've never been baptized in the Holy Spirit, I encourage you to ask the Holy Spirit to fill you now with His love, His heart and His power for living life well. Write today's date here so you can remember the anniversary of your Baptism. Also, journal anything the Holy Spirit shows you here.

_____
_____
_____
_____
_____
_____
_____
_____
_____
_____
_____
_____

Romans 14:7-8 says, "For none of us lives to himself, and no one dies to himself. For if we live, we live to the Lord; and if we die, we die to the Lord. Therefore, whether we live or die, we are the Lord's." We are here on this planet to love Him, love others, and bring Heaven to earth through the unique gifts He's given us. In this life, our natural state should be peace and joy. Walking out your destiny will give you the most satisfaction in life. If you're saved but you've never asked Jesus to be your Lord, now is a great day to make a Lordship commitment. Commit to following and obeying Him. Write today's date here and ask Him if He has anything to show you. Journal here.

God loves to celebrate! He loves the feasts of Israel and loves time. I got saved April 13, 1997 and every year since, I celebrate my spiritual birthday with the Lord and He gives me a present. When I got baptized in the Holy Spirit in 2002 at church, I didn't write the date down so later all I knew is it was in the fall. October 6, 2015 I woke up hearing the Holy Spirit say, "Happy birthday, Annie!" I didn't know what He was talking about because my natural birthday is in July, my spiritual birthday is in April and this was a morning in October. It occurred to me that if October 6, 2002 was a Sunday, that He was telling me that was my Holy Spirit birthday. I looked the date up online and sure enough it was a Sunday! God gave me an entire week of presents, including a suddenly of Lasik eye surgery, a new iPhone and a few other things.

PRAYER ACTIVATION

The Lord loves your relationship with Him and is always looking to celebrate the gift of you! Journal any significant dates here that you and the Lord can celebrate your relationship together.

Waging War with Prophetic Words

As you begin to get prophetic words and the Lord shows you who you are and what you're called to do, you'll need to "wage war" with these words. The Apostle Paul exhorted his spiritual son, Timothy in 1 Timothy 1:18-19, "This charge I commit to you, son Timothy, according to the prophecies previously made concerning you, that by them you may wage the good warfare, having faith and good conscience,". Waging war with your words means to declare them aloud and meditate on them so that faith is built in your heart to walk them out.

Psalm 105:19 explains the preparation process of God concerning prophetic words, "Until the time that his word came to pass, the word of the Lord tested him." In Genesis 37-50, God tells us the story of Joseph's life. In chapter 37 when Joseph is a teenager, God gives him dreams of his future greatness. Joseph is quite arrogant in sharing what God has shown him to his brothers and in their jealousy and rage, they throw Joseph into a pit and then sell him into slavery. He experiences future injustice and is thrown into prison. After thirteen years have passed where God has worked on refining Joseph's character in the midst of trials and tribulations, Joseph is promoted into leadership and walks out the prophetic destiny God spoke over his life years before. When you receive your prophetic words, they carry the ability to mold you into the person capable of walking out the prophesied destiny. It's usually a process. Moses spent 40 years in the backside of the desert becoming the deliverer that God promised he would be. Our process doesn't have to be as difficult as Joseph's was if we submit to the Lord and embrace our preparation and refining process.

PRAYER ACTIVATION

Ask God where you are in the process of development in your journey. Write down your prophetic words (that came from God personally or from another person) that you're committing to wage war with. There's a benefit of taking your words and writing a statement of declaration to proclaim over your life.

_____
_____
_____
_____
_____
_____
_____
_____
_____
_____
_____
_____

There is a tension between living with the realization of Revelation 19:10 "the testimony of Jesus is the spirit of prophecy" and receiving prophetic words given to other people. The testimony of Jesus being the spirit of prophecy means that what Jesus has done for one person, He'll do for another because as Acts 10:34-35 says, "Then Peter opened his mouth and said: "In truth I perceive that God shows no partiality. But in every nation whoever fears Him and works righteousness is accepted by Him."" This concept is a faith builder for people, especially in receiving healing and salvation. But they can erroneously transfer this notion into receiving prophetic words that they hear for other people. If you need a healing and you hear a word saying God is healing that person, by all means, receive it as God's heart to heal, let it build your faith, and receive your healing. But if you hear a word that God is giving someone business ideas to make millions of dollars for the Kingdom, if you're not called to the business arena or called to steward millions of dollars, please don't receive that word. We're each accountable for bearing fruit from our talents so if you're receiving words that are not for you and that you're not equipped to walk in, you're taking on responsibility that you don't have the grace to walk out. Stay in your lane, trust God to speak to you and to give you the prophetic words He wants to give you, and celebrate others and their prophetic words. The only time I receive prophetic words that are given to others is if the Holy Spirit quickens them to me and tells me personally that they're also for me. Other than that, I celebrate people and allow them to have the specific word from God that He's given them. On the one or two occasions that's happened, I'll write the word in my journal as a faith builder but not a word that I wage war with. I trust God to give me my own words, either from Him personally or through a prophetic word that I need and I encourage others to do the same.

PRAYER ACTIVATION

Ask the Lord if there are any words you received over your life that He didn't intend for you to steward. If so, lay them down. Journal what the Lord says to you here.

_____
_____
_____
_____
_____
_____
_____
_____
_____

Power in Ministering Through the Eye Gates

There is power in ministering with your eyes to another person. When you allow the Holy Spirit to look through your eyes with love, much can be accomplished without words being spoken. This is especially helpful when you're in a social or public setting and you're not able to minister to someone. I'll know when the Lord is ministering through my eyes because often the person will comment on the uniqueness or beauty of my eyes. They may not have language for it but they're supernaturally receiving from God through looking into my eyes.

I recently ministered to a 13-year-old girl and her family. As I looked at her face and neck, I saw she looked light green, similar to the Wicked Witch in the Wizard of Oz, but many shades lighter. I initially thought she'd done her makeup perfectly in a light green shade and wondered why she'd want to look like that. Then I realized that what I was seeing was not in the natural but in the spiritual so I asked God what the color was about. He told me it was a spirit of death attacking her, along with a spirit of rebellion. I asked Him how to go about ministering to her. I didn't want to scare her or her parents, yet I knew the situation was dire. I felt God saying to tell her to read Deuteronomy 18. I told her that I felt God was saying she needed to read Deuteronomy 18 because the chapter is about the blessings of choosing life. She nodded as I said that. I encouraged her again that it's her choice and it's important to choose life. She said she understood. In addition, I asked God what her future was about and what the call on her life held. He said she has an evangelistic gift that will bring millions of souls into the Kingdom and that that is what the enemy is terrified about. I prophesied to her and told her that she will bring millions of souls into the Kingdom by choosing life. I told her that those souls hung in the balance if she chose life. She again said she understood. Then I looked deep into her eyes and allowed my spirit and the Holy Spirit to reveal truth to her but I didn't say any other words. Her mother sat next to us, quietly crying. I knew by the Spirit that her mother was an intercessor and was on her knees crying out for her daughter's salvation and safety. Throughout the ministry time, I stared into the girl's eyes for nearly 5 minutes. I knew the Lord was doing a deep work in her. After I was finished ministering, I walked away and I spoke out loud binding the spirit of death in the girl's life. I released life to her and knew that it may be a process and a journey but that death would not be allowed to take her.

I encourage you to be intentional in looking into people's eyes and releasing the love of the Father to them. We are privileged to know Him and know His love and want to invite others into relationship with Him.

PRAYER ACTIVATION

I invite you here to journal and receive more of the Father's love for yourself and for the world around them. "Father, I ask for more of Your love. Fill me with more of You and the revelation of You and Your heart for me and for the world." I also encourage you to declare Ephesians 1:17-19 over yourself now, "that the God of our Lord Jesus Christ, the Father of glory, may give to me the spirit of wisdom and revelation in the knowledge of Him, the eyes of my understanding being enlightened; that I may know what is the hope of His calling, what are the riches of the glory of His inheritance in the saints, and what is the exceeding greatness of His power toward us who believe."

_____
_____
_____
_____
_____
_____
_____
_____
_____
_____
_____
_____
_____
_____
_____
_____

God's Ways

CHAPTER 4

PROPHETIC JOURNEYS WITH GOD

It honors God when we seek to know His heart and His ways. Psalm 103:7 tells us, "He made known His ways to Moses, His acts to the children of Israel." The children of Israel did not know God intimately, so they only knew what He did and the miracles He performed. Moses pursued God's heart and God showed him not only what He does but His heart behind His actions. King David, a man after God's own heart describes God to us in Psalm 103:1-6, "Bless the Lord, O my soul; and all that is within me, bless His holy name! Bless the Lord, O my soul, and forget not all His benefits: Who forgives all your iniquities, Who heals all your diseases, Who redeems your life from destruction, Who crowns you with loving kindness and tender mercies, Who satisfies your mouth with good things, so that your youth is renewed like the eagle's. The Lord executes righteousness and justice for all who are oppressed."

God wants to draw us into an intimate friendship with Him. He wants to teach us to love Him well. Throughout the history of mankind, God's heart has been to pursue intimacy with His creation and teach them His ways. Enoch was the great grandfather of Noah and Hebrews 11:5 testifies of his great love for God, 'By faith Enoch was taken away so that he did not see death, "and was not found, because

God had taken him"; for before he was taken he had this testimony, that he pleased God.' Enoch walked so closely with God that when he was 365 years old, God took him to heaven to be with Him without Enoch first dying.

Abraham, the father of faith, was known as a friend of God. There is no higher calling than to be friends with God. Genesis 12:1-3 recounts the story of God appearing to Abram (his name before God renamed him Abraham in chapter 17:5), 'Now the Lord had said to Abram: "Get out of your country, from your family and from your father's house, to a land that I will show you. I will make you a great nation; I will bless you and make your name great; and you shall be a blessing. I will bless those who bless you, and I will curse him who curses you; and in you all the families of the earth shall be blessed."' Abraham's obedience and willingness to follow God on a prophetic journey earned him the honor of being named the father of faith. Hebrews 11:8-9 recounts the story of Abraham's faithfulness to God, "By faith Abraham obeyed when he was called to go out to the place which he would receive as an inheritance. And he went out, not knowing where he was going. By faith he dwelt in the land of promise as in a foreign country, dwelling in tents with Isaac and Jacob, the heirs with him of the same promise; for he waited for the city which has foundations, whose builder and maker is God."

It is our choice in our life whether we want to know God's ways or God's acts. This is what God has to say about the people of Israel who wandered around the desert for forty years because they were rebellious in Psalms 95:8-11, "Do not harden your hearts, as in the rebellion, as in the day of trial in the wilderness, when your fathers tested Me; they tried Me, though they saw My work. For forty years I was grieved with that generation, and said, 'It is a people who go astray in their hearts, and they do not know My ways.' So I swore in My wrath, 'They shall not enter My rest.'"

PRAYER ACTIVATION

Take some time here to examine your heart. Do you know God's ways or God's acts in your life? Have you had a hardened heart? If so, take some time to repent and commit to spending the rest of your life learning God's ways. Journal your thoughts and God's response here.

_____
_____
_____
_____
_____
_____
_____
_____
_____
_____
_____
_____
_____
_____
_____
_____

My husband, Joe, and I have told God that we will live our lives for Him and will teach our children to do the same. We've found that God loves faith and has trained us in many faith journeys in our walk with Him. My first prophetic journey with God began a few years after I was saved. I was learning to hear His voice and this was the first time I stepped out with action for what I believed He was saying to me. I was pregnant with our second daughter, Grace, in 2000. Joe and I were finishing our M.B.A. graduate degrees and timed the pregnancy for the birth to occur after graduation. We, surprisingly, became pregnant the first month we tried to conceive. This put my due date at the end of July, 2000. My own birthday is July 23 and I, unexpectedly to me, delivered my first daughter, Madeleine on July 23, 1998. She was five days early and it had not occurred to me that I would share a birthday with a child. After our ultrasound in March 2000 to determine that our second child was a girl, I began to talk to God about when Grace would be born. After much thought, I decided that Grace might feel left out if Mommy and Madeleine shared a birthday and her own birthday was a few days later. I asked God what He thought about it. I felt He told me that if I had faith that Grace would be born seven days early on July 23 to share the birthday, she would indeed be born that day. I thought about it through the early summer months and decided that I could believe God for that special birthday present. I had a long difficult labor with Madeleine in 1998 that began on the 22nd and ended with her birth 20 hours later on the 23rd. I was not expecting her that early and consequently, did not celebrate my own birthday that year. I was disappointed by that and didn't want to miss another celebration. I also did not have faith that I would have a short labor with my second birth so I knew that labor would likely need to begin again on the 22nd for me to deliver on the 23rd. In faith, and with some doubt, I made plans to go out for a birthday dinner for Madeleine and me on the evening of the 22nd with Joe and family. I told God that contractions could start after dessert and that I would then be ready to have a birthday baby. I cleaned my house, had the nursery ready, packed my hospital bags, had my hair done and a pedicure before going for dinner on the 22nd. While eating dessert, contractions began. On the drive home from the restaurant, it became obvious that I was in labor. My in-laws offered to have Madeleine spend the night with them and I gave them her pre-packed bag. Joe and I then went home to pick up our bags. At this point it was 10:00 pm and contractions stopped. I went right to bed so that I could get some rest. I slept on Madeleine's bed because it had a water proof mattress pad on it. When Joe came to bed with me at midnight, I had just awakened because contractions began in earnest. We lived an hour away from the hospital but I didn't want to make the drive until I knew for sure that I was going to have the baby. I was still laying in bed at 2:00 am with contractions that were not strong enough to go to the hospital but were painful enough to keep me from falling back to sleep. At that point, I felt tired and began to wonder if I was wrong about hearing God about the shared birthday. I prayed and told God that I was sorry if I had been presumptuous, and if that was the case, asked Him if He would make the contractions stop. Then I asked Him if this was really the beginning of my having my second daughter on my birthday, that He would give me a sign. I felt peace wash over me and literally five seconds later my water broke. I woke Joe up to drive to the hospital. Grace Ann was born 19 hours later at 9:11 pm on July 23, 2000. We have had wonderful birthday celebrations through the years and the faith journey with God taught me God's heart and His ways. I will forever give Him glory for the miracle of the shared birthdays.

Walking through the journey believing God for a specific birthday prepared me for longer journeys of believing God for His promises to manifest. When He spoke to us, we moved from Michigan to Redding, California and then when He spoke again 8 years later, we moved to Raleigh, North Carolina at His direction. We have experienced many other faith journeys with God through the years. Each one takes faith, challenges belief, does not always make the most practical sense, but always yields the fruit of pleasing God.

PRAYER ACTIVATION

Record here any faith journeys you've taken with God. Is He currently wooing your heart to go on another one with Him that you haven't yet said yes to?

_____
_____
_____
_____
_____
_____
_____
_____
_____
_____
_____
_____
_____
_____

In Luke 19:16-19, Jesus is telling the parable of the talents, "Then came the first, saying, 'Master, your mina has earned ten minas.' And he said to him, 'Well done, good servant; because you were faithful in a very little, have authority over ten cities.' And the second came, saying, 'Master, your mina has earned five minas.' Likewise, he said to him, 'You also be over five cities.'" When we're faithful to steward our lives well, God is pleased and give us authority over more. We have friends who are faithful to obey the Lord and know His voice. When He asks them to move to another city, they obey, even if they don't know why He is moving them. In the span of a twenty-four-month period, God moved them three times. They lived in four states; the eastern and western states bordered the Atlantic and Pacific Oceans. The northern and southern states bordered Canada and Mexico. Each move was expensive and didn't seem to make logical sense but they followed the voice of the Lord. A year after they arrived and settled in the fourth state, God spoke to them to tell them what He had accomplished through their radical obedience. He told them He was giving them authority over the nation of the United States and He accomplished it through them living in the west, east, north and south. Their story is still unfolding so they don't know what their having authority over the nation yet entails but they've dedicated their lives to saying yes to God's ways.

Prophetic Journals

God loves prophesying our year to us and loves playing with us. Each year God's New Year begins at the Jewish festival Rosh Hashana in the fall. My friends and I put together prophetic journals each year to have fun with God and prophesy our year. We get together with composition books, lots of magazines, scissors, glue, and lots of food. We flip through the magazines and cut out what is highlighted to us by the Holy Spirit. It may be pictures or words and it's not necessarily things we're interested in or even enjoy. Then, when we feel we each have all the things cut out, we individually arrange them on the covers of our composition books and glue them in place. The composites are creative and interesting. Throughout the next year, events will happen in our lives that God prophesied through the prophetic journals. I began doing the journals with my students at Catch the Fire's School of Revelation, as well as many of the ladies from Catch the Fire. It's part of learning to play with God and a tool for prophetic journeys with God.

Some of my favorite testimonies from the journals have occurred in the past year. On my personal journal in the fall of 2016 was the promise of buying a new house for our family. It was something we've been praying into and believing the Lord for. Sure enough, June of 2017, we bought a new home and realized the goodness of God and the completion of a prophetic journey with Him.

Our church is the home base for an amazing young woman missionary to the Amazon rain forest. She spends most of the year planting churches and overseeing the churches in the Amazon. She loves the people there and loves most of her life there, except she's been bothered by not being able to shave her legs unless she's on furlough in Raleigh. This past year, while making her journal, God highlighted the words, "laser hair removal". She cut out the words and glued them to an inside page and didn't think much about them. A few months later, a good friend who owns a medical health spa invited the young missionary to come see her at her office. The missionary didn't know what the medical spa did but went to visit her friend. When she got to the office, the receptionist told the missionary that her friend had arranged to provide her with laser hair removal. The missionary was stunned that God had orchestrated an answer to a desire of her heart and that it had been prophesied for her year in her prophetic journal.

One of my students, while doing her journal last year, saw a picture of an industrial sized sewing machine highlighted to her. She cut it out and glued it onto her journal. Her heart is to help women who have been sex trafficked get free and integrate back into society. Nine months after completing her journal, the student took a job teaching sewing lessons to women who have been rescued from sex slavery. She was amazed by God's heart and intentionality towards her and her year.

If you've never done a prophetic journal, it's a very fun way to play with God and learn His ways. I encourage you to do a journal each year and to say yes to walking with Him on faith journeys throughout your life.

God's Ways

CHAPTER 5

ANGELS

Scripture is full of reference to angels and their role in the earth. Let's examine their purposes on a journey through the Bible:

Angel's are God's servants. They get their instructions from hearing the written and spoken Word of God. They then go help accomplish the assignment.

Psalm 103:20: "Bless the Lord, you His angels, mighty in strength, who perform His word, obeying the voice of His word!"

Hebrews 1:7: "And of the angels He says, "Who makes His angels winds, and His ministers a flame of fire."

Hebrews 1:14: "Are they not all ministering spirits, sent out to render service for the sake of those who will inherit salvation?"

Numbers 20:16: "But when we cried out to the Lord, He heard our voice and sent an angel and brought us out from Egypt; now behold, we are at Kadesh, a town on the edge of your territory."

Angels protect people. We cry out to the Lord and He sends angels to our cause. We don't command angels. God does. We ask Him for angelic help.

Psalm 91:11-12: "For He shall give His angels charge over you, to keep you in all your ways. In their hands they shall bear you up, lest you dash your foot against a stone."

Matthew 26:52-53: "Put your sword in its place, for all who take the sword will perish by the sword. Or do you think that I cannot now pray to My Father, and He will provide Me with more than twelve legions of angels?"

Acts 5:19: "But during the night an angel of the Lord opened the gates of the prison."

Angels worship God, just like people do. They join in when the people of God praise Him.

Psalm 148:2: "Praise Him, all His angels; Praise Him, all His hosts!"

Angels deliver messages from God, in person and in dreams. We don't worship angels. Seeing them can make us afraid because of the awe and reverence they bring. They commune with God in the throne room of Heaven and carry a very strong presence/fragrance of the Lord.

Luke 1:11-13: 'Then an angel of the Lord appeared to him, standing on the right side of the altar of incense. And when Zacharias saw him, he was troubled, and fear fell upon him. But the angel said to him, "Do not be afraid, Zacharias, for your prayer is heard; and your wife Elizabeth will bear you a son, and you shall call his name John."'

Luke 1:28-31: 'And having come in, the angel said to her, "Rejoice, highly favored one, the Lord is with you; blessed are you among women!" But when she saw him, she was troubled at his saying, and considered what manner of greeting this was. Then the angel said to her, "Do not be afraid, Mary, for you have found favor with God. And behold, you will conceive in your womb and bring forth a Son, and shall call His name Jesus."'

Matthew 1:20-21: 'But while he thought about these things, behold, an angel of the Lord appeared to him in a dream, saying, "Joseph, son of David, do not be afraid to take to you Mary your wife, for that which is conceived in her is of the Holy Spirit. And she will bring forth a Son, and you shall call His name Jesus, for He will save His people from their sins."'

Matthew 2:13: 'Now when they had departed, behold, an angel of the Lord appeared to Joseph in a dream, saying, "Arise, take the young Child and His mother, flee to Egypt, and stay there until I bring you word; for Herod will seek the young Child to destroy Him."'

Numbers 22:21-35: 'So Balaam arose in the morning, and saddled his donkey and went with the leaders of Moab. But God was angry because he was going, and the angel of the Lord took his stand in the way as an adversary against him. Now he was riding on his donkey and his two servants were with him. When the donkey saw the angel of the Lord standing in the way with his drawn sword in his hand, the donkey turned off from the way and went into the field; but Balaam struck the donkey to turn her back into the way. Then the angel of the Lord stood in a narrow path of the vineyards, with a wall on this side and a wall on that side. When the donkey saw the angel of the Lord, she pressed herself to the wall and pressed Balaam's foot against the wall, so he struck her again. The angel of the Lord went further, and stood in a narrow place where there was no way to turn to the right hand or the left. When the donkey saw the angel of the Lord, she lay down under Balaam; so Balaam was angry and struck the donkey with his stick. And the Lord opened the mouth of the donkey, and she said to Balaam, "What have I done to you, that you have struck me these three times?" Then Balaam said to the donkey, "Because you have made a mockery of me! If there had been a sword in my hand, I would have killed you by now." The donkey said to Balaam, "Am I not your donkey on which you have ridden all your life to this day? Have I ever been accustomed to do so to you?" And he said, "No." Then the Lord opened the eyes of Balaam, and he saw the angel of the Lord standing in the way with his drawn sword in his hand; and he bowed all the way to the ground. The angel of the Lord said to him, "Why have you struck your donkey these three times? Behold, I have come out as an adversary, because your way was contrary to me. "But the donkey saw me and turned aside from me these three times. If she had not turned aside from me, I would surely have killed you just now, and let her live." Balaam said to the angel of the Lord, "I have sinned, for I did not know that you were standing in the way against me. Now then, if it is displeasing to you, I will turn back." But the angel of the Lord said to Balaam, "Go with the men, but you shall speak only the word which I tell you." So Balaam went along with the leaders of Balak.'

Angels war the demonic on our behalf. As they war to bring about God's solutions, we are required to pray and fast and worship and employ all the other Kingdom tools we have. These verses in Daniel show us what happens behind the veil. Daniel fasted and prayed for three weeks asking God to answer his prayer. The angel that appeared with the answer three weeks after Daniel began to pray explained what happened. He said he left with the answer as soon as Daniel began to pray but the demonic battled him and tried to abort God's solution. A high level demonic, the prince from Persia, battled the angel. There was gridlock in the battle until God sent the archangel, Michael. to help the angel defeat the prince from Persia. Then the angel brought to Daniel God's answer. Our prayers empower the angels to war on our behalf. How many times have we stopped praying and therefore, the demonic stopped God's intervention in our lives?

Daniel 10:2-3: "In those days I, Daniel, was mourning three full weeks. I ate no pleasant food, no meat or wine came into my mouth, nor did I anoint myself at all, till three whole weeks were fulfilled."

Daniel 10:10-13: 'Suddenly, a hand touched me, which made me tremble, on my knees and on the palms of my hands. And he said to me, "O Daniel, man greatly beloved, understand the words that I speak to you, and stand upright, for I have now been sent to you." While he was speaking this word to me, I stood trembling. Then he said to me, "Do not fear, Daniel, for from the first day that you set your heart to understand, and to humble yourself before your God, your words were heard; and I have come because of your words. But the prince of the kingdom of Persia was withstanding me for twenty-one days; then behold, Michael, one of the chief princes, came to help me, for I had been left there with the kings of Persia."'

PRAYER ACTIVATION

Ask God if there is something He wants to release to you and ask Him what the prayer strategy is to see it come to pass. Journal here.

_____

_____

Everyone has a guardian angel who helps to protect them. In addition, there are lots of angels on assignment in churches, homes, businesses and other places. We're surrounded by God's warriors and messengers. How do we be intentional about identifying them and working with them? First, understanding their purpose and how they respond to God's word, whether it's spoken Scripture, prayer or a prophetic declaration, is helpful. You can have faith that God will send them on assignment for you as you partner with Him.

Just like with anything in the spiritual realm, we can discern a lot through our spiritual senses. I often sense the presence of the Holy Spirit hovering over me. He feels like a warm, heavy, vibrating blanket. He brings refreshing and healing and joy. The Holy Spirit vibrates at a faster frequency than the angels do. The feeling of sitting in a hot tub with the bubbles on high is similar to what spiritual vibrations feel like in the air. Angels in the atmosphere will emit a frequency that I can "feel" and therefore, know where they are in a room.

I can also sometimes "see" angels. They appear in many different ways: flashes of light flying by (similar to a shooting star), shimmering lights (similar to seeing heat waves on pavement), twinkle lights (I call these "twinkle" angels. They appear and await your declaration. Then they fly off to accomplish it. They often appear in the shower or during mundane tasks.), parts or all of the angels show up to the natural eye (often at night, looking translucent like a hologram). In my experience thus far, when angels show up in part or completely visible to the naked eye, they're here to bring a message, instruction from God, a healing, or an impartation. I've also seen things that I can't explain: clouds of red mist, screens with blue ink coming from them, white clouds of mist, and other things.

Another way to "see" angels is to look around a room with your spiritual eyes. The screen that God uses for us to see spiritually is the screen of our imaginations. If I tell you to close your eyes and imagine a pink elephant, you can see it on your spiritual screen. When you look around a room, even with your natural eyes open, and pay attention to your spiritual screen, you can see imprints of what's in the spiritual atmosphere around you. Almost like when the flash of a camera goes off and you "see" the room briefly, that's what it can look like. There's a lot of activity in a room, especially places where people worship. In my living room, I've seen waterfalls, angels, portals, and other things.

Often during the night in the dark, I'll awake because of the angelic activity in the room. I'll see things with my natural eyes wide open. My favorite spiritual sighting was a bright purple and mallard green colored miniature humming bird type bird. I've seen it flying in my room on two occasions. It's the most beautiful thing I've ever seen. It looked like a literal tiny bird flying around my room. It was not translucent. I don't know why it was there but it carried the fragrance and frequency of Heaven.

A few times during the night, angels have appeared at my bedside and given me wisdom and instruction. One night, I was very tired, but God asked me to intercede for a couple in our church. He woke me up twice to pray and told me it was a spirit of suicide after them. I fell back asleep twice. The third time, an angel appeared at my bedside, woke me up and very sternly commanded me to get out of bed and go pray. I quickly got out of bed, told God I was sorry, and went to pray for the couple.

Another way to discern an angel is when there is a frequency shift in your ear. Usually it's just one ear, although it doesn't seem to matter which ear. It sounds like a gear shifting to a higher gear in your ear but it's more of a sensation than a sound. When I experience that, I'll ask God if there's anything I need to pray. Often it's just an angel manifesting in the atmosphere or bringing a healing.

Sometimes an angel will touch a person's head or body to release God's healing. When God wants to rewire a person's thought process, heal a trauma, renew his/her mind and such, an angel will touch a person's head. It can feel like tingling in that one spot or heat. Other times, when angels stand next to me, that side of my body will tingle and feel heat. If I happen to bump into them, it can feel like bumping into a solid object, yet nothing appears to be there. Also, sometimes they fly away suddenly and it feels like a whirlwind where they were.

When I was growing up, there were many times I would have a sensation that is difficult to describe. I have no idea if it would last a few seconds or a few hours. I would only feel it as I came out of the experience. It felt completely loving, relaxing, like being suspended in warm water. Each time, I would feel energized, loved, refreshed and emotionally healed. A few years after I got saved, I was at church at a worship evening with Rita Springer. As I stood worshiping, the experience from my childhood happened. I was conscious of it the entire time. In amazement, I asked God what it was. He told me it was the Seraphim angels. He said He would send them to me for protection and healing throughout my growing up years. When He said that, I felt so loved and cherished by Him.

PRAYER ACTIVATION

As you read through this section on identifying angels, have you had similar encounters or did this give language to what you've already experienced? I release an impartation now for you to discern the angelic and the atmosphere of Heaven and for you to partner well with God's kingdom. I encourage you to write today's date and journal here.

_____

_____

_____

_____

_____

_____

Spiritual Warfare in Dreams

People commonly experience spiritual warfare in dreams. I wrote a chapter on how to practically interpret dreams in my workbook, *Everlasting Prophetic: Bridging Heaven to Earth*. It's very helpful in growing in interpretation. In addition, I highly recommend Dr. Barbie Breathitt's *A to Z Dream Symbology Dictionary*. It has the possible spiritual meaning of ten thousand common symbols God uses to speak to people in dreams.

If you have a dream that feels negative and like warfare, for example, a snake biting you or a shark or alligator chasing you, I recommend praying through it like this: "I cancel the assignment of the enemy against me, in Jesus name. I pray for complete protection over me and my family and Father, I ask You to heal any areas of my life that need healing and alignment with You." By you praying through the dream, God is able to intervene in your life with His solutions.

A friend of mine had a dream where she saw her boss begin to hand her a present and then seemingly change his mind and withdraw the present. When she awoke, God instructed her to pray through the dream by changing the outcome of the dream. She prayed through it while she was awake by imagining the picture of her boss. Instead of him withdrawing the present, she imagined him handing the present to her and him being overjoyed as she opened it. The next morning after she'd prayed through the dream with God, her boss gave her a significant promotion and raise! Changing the outcome of dreams so that real life reflects the change must be done with caution and through partnering with the Holy Spirit so that we don't partner with a spirit of control, witchcraft and manipulation.

PRAYER ACTIVATION

Spend a few minutes with God now and pray through any dreams that need His help and resolution for your life. Journal here.

_____
_____
_____
_____
_____

God's Ways

CHAPTER 6

7 MOUNTAINS

Jesus commissioned us with last instructions before He ascended to Heaven after His resurrection. In Matthew 28:18-20 (The Passion Translation) we're commanded, 'Then Jesus came close to them and said, "All the authority of the universe has been given to me. Now go in my authority and make disciples of all nations, baptizing them in the name of the Father, the Son, and the Holy Spirit. And teach them to faithfully follow all that I have commanded you. And never forget that I AM with you every day, even to the completion of this age."'

Discipling nations, not just preaching the Gospel of salvation, is God's plan for Believers. God's way is for us to bring Heaven to earth in all of society. The culture of Heaven is one of freedom. Freedom to choose whom to worship. Everyone who resides with God in Heaven chose to worship Him. The angels who chose to rebel are no longer in heaven. Understanding that freedom is a huge value to God, we need to base our model of discipling nations here on freedom. As God and man give us favor to influence, if we represent God's heart of love and honor properly, people are free to choose His kingdom.

Os Hillman of 7culturalmountains.org explains the origin and the strategy of God in discipling nations. "There are 7 Mountains of influence in culture. In 1975, Bill Bright, founder of Campus Crusade, and Loren Cunningham, founder of Youth With a Mission, had lunch together in Colorado. God simultaneously gave each of these change agents a message to give to the other. During that same time frame, Francis Schaeffer was given a similar message. That message was that if we are to impact any nation for Jesus Christ, then we would have to affect the seven spheres, or mountains of society that are the pillars of any society. These seven mountains are business, government, media, arts and entertainment, education, the family, and religion. There are many subgroups under these main categories. About a month later, the Lord showed Francis Schaeffer the same thing. In essence, God was telling these three change agents where the battlefield was. It was here where culture would be won or lost. Their assignment was to raise up change agents to scale the mountains and to help a new generation of change agents understand the larger story. The 7 mountains initiative is not an initiative to establish dominion over all the earth or in governments. It is an initiative that seeks to love and serve all people on the earth. As followers of Christ, we believe we are called to love all people, regardless of faith, lifestyle or gender orientation. God loves all people. He provides guidelines for living as found in the Holy Scriptures and we support those guidelines as a people called to love and obey His calling upon our lives. Jesus invites all people into this destiny, but not all will come. We are called to model what Christ taught when He prayed that what was in Heaven would be manifested on earth through a people known for their love of one another and others. That means His love and grace would be extended to all people."

An important point about discipling nations is that we're not called to dominate cities or nations like the Emperor Constantine did in AD 313 or how John Calvin did in Geneva, Switzerland in the 1500s. Unbelievers and even Believers who didn't agree with Calvin's doctrine were executed. We're called to influence, to love and serve and help our cities, not impose rule over them. It's been proven throughout history that it's not possible to legislate morality. Rather, winning the hearts of people in culture through service and kingdom solutions, will disciple nations. Jesus never imposed His will over anyone. He always gave them freedom to choose. That needs to be our model. When we demonstrate the heart of the Father and Jesus' ability to bring life and life more abundantly, people can't help but choose to worship Him, in all His glory.

As Believers, we owe the world an encounter with God, that they would know His goodness, His majesty, His love. Our individual discovery of whom He made us to be and which of the 7 mountains we're called to impact can bring His solutions to a hurting planet. We carry the mind of Christ to solve problems, the anointing of the Holy Spirit to bring His love. We should be diligent to develop our gifts and do all things with joy and excellence. As we do, we look different from the world and it makes people hungry to know our Father. I saw a movie last summer that illustrates how different we are as believers when we approach the ills of society. It was called "Beatriz at Dinner". The movie highlighted the evils of business people caring more about money than people, as well as aspects about friendship, loyalty, and physical healing. What struck me is it literally carried no anointing of the Holy Spirit that I could discern, and therefore, no answers or hope to resolving life's problems. I honestly don't remember the last time I saw a movie that wasn't overtly sinful like this one that carried zero anointing. The box office gross of a mere $7 million confirmed the fact that people are looking for anointed solutions and hope for the world's problems and recognize lack of hope and wisdom when they see it. Movies that aren't overtly Christian, yet carry the anointing of the Holy Spirit, achieve worldwide phenomenal success. The gross earnings of Schindler's List ($321 million), The Matrix ($463 million), Brave heart ($210 million), The Chronicles of

Narnia ($745 million) prove that providing hope and a future in culture win the hearts of the people. Wonder Woman ($821 million), Spiderman ($821 million), and The Avengers ($1.5 billion) prove that people want to see justice and righteousness and strong people as heroes. People intrinsically recognize that we're all called to be great in God's kingdom. Interestingly enough, the movie Avatar grossed $2.7 billion. Even as I watched it years ago, my heart leapt and was drawn to the colors and the scenery and the cry of the heart to be deeply "seen". I knew that the movie portrayed a glimpse of Heaven, of the love and the vibrant colors that we'll experience there. Obviously, that movie touched the hearts of many, whether they understood why or not.

Just like in the above mentioned movies, we, as God's people, have the opportunity to be super heroes of our day to bring love, hope and a future to the world. When we carry the wisdom of the Holy Spirit and the love of God, people will recognize the kingdom we come from and want to be a part of it, too.

We have to recognize that even as we do our best, there will still be nations that don't choose Kingdom ways and people that won't choose salvation through Christ. In the Passion Translation, Matthew 25:31-34 describes this reality, "When the Son of Man appears in his majestic glory, with all his angels by his side, he will take his seat on the throne of splendor, and all the nations will be gathered together before him. And like a shepherd who separates the sheep from the goats, he will separate all the people. The 'sheep' he will put on his right side and the 'goats' on his left. Then the King will turn to those on his right and say, 'You have a special place in my Father's heart. Come and experience the full inheritance of the kingdom realm that has been destined for you from before the foundation of the world.'" However, it is still our responsibility to do the absolute best we can for Jesus to get His full reward.

I believe that God has given individuals, cities, states, and nations individual identities that reflect glorious aspects of His nature. As we discover these identities, and call them into them, God will receive the glory due to Him.

Habakkuk 2:14: "For the whole earth will be filled with the knowledge of the glory of the Lord, as the waters cover the sea." This verse conveys the message of the 7 mountain theology better than just the message of salvation. I highly recommend reading Johnny Enlow's book, *The Seven Mountain Renaissance: Vision and Strategy through 2050*. He says that this renaissance will be about "The Brilliance of God on Display" whereas the previous renaissance from the fourteenth century to the seventeenth century was about the brilliance of man. Enlow describes this new renaissance by saying on pp 25-26, "What will mark the new Era of Renaissance in which we are now living? There will be such an increase in the knowledge of God and His ways that life on earth will be changed forever. Generally, when Christians think of Habakkuk 2:14 or of the reality of the knowledge of God covering the earth, they think of it in terms of people knowing that God saves. Though that is a most wonderful thing---God sent His only begotten Son, Jesus, to offer salvation to whosoever would repent and receive Him---it is clearly evident that this perspective restricts "knowledge of God" to only one aspect of who He is. The knowledge of God cannot be limited to only the knowledge that He saves. Part of the beauty of the Seven Mountain message is that it proclaims a God who not only saves (Mountain of Religion) but also governs (Mountain of Government), is creative (Mountain of Celebration/Arts), is a Communications Expert (Mountain of Media), is our Father, or "Papa" (Mountain of Family), is our Provider (Mountain of Economy), and is our Teacher (Mountain of Education). Beyond these seven primary expressions of who God is lies an additional array of many hills of secondary aspects of His character that He desires to reveal to us. This Era of Renaissance that we have entered into will not be complete until the invisible God is made visible through the lives of His ambassadorial kids in every area of society. That's what the above verse means when it says "as the waters cover the sea." It will be a full saturation of knowledge that covers every nook and cranny of society. Jesus will not return until He has filled the whole earth with an understanding of God's amazing ways of doing everything."

I don't know about you but reading Johnny Enlow's book and hearing teachers like Lance Walnau, John Maxwell and others discuss the plan of God for His glory to fill the earth excites me! This is the discipling nations strategy that God wants us to employ with love and wisdom. Every Believer is called to play a part. No one sits on the bench, every one plays.

PRAYER ACTIVATION

If you've never heard this concept before, I suggest you study and get it into your thought process. Please take some time with God and ask Him which mountain(s) you're personally called to influence and serve in. Also, ask Him for specific direction for your life regarding your service and any preparation that you need. (Mountains are Religion, Government, Celebration/Arts, Media, Family, Economy, Education.)

_____
_____
_____
_____
_____
_____

God's Voice

CHAPTER 7

Scripture! Scripture! Scripture!

It's critical as a prophetic Believer to be grounded in the truth of Scripture. Let me say that again. It's absolutely critical as a prophetic Believer to be grounded in the truth of Scripture. Having a solid foundation in the knowledge of Scripture and reading the Bible regularly is what will keep you stable throughout your Christian walk. "So then faith comes by hearing, and hearing by the word of God," Romans 10:17. This verse means that our faith is built upon hearing/reading/knowing the word of God in Scripture but that continual hearing is necessary to build our faith.

Jesus is the Word of God. Loving Jesus means loving the Bible. John 1:1-5 reveals Jesus, "In the beginning was the Word, and the Word was with God, and the Word was God. He was in the beginning with God. All things were made through Him, and without Him nothing was made that was made. In Him was life, and the life was the light of men. And the light shines in the darkness, and the darkness did not comprehend it." You can't love Jesus without loving Scripture because Jesus is the Word of God.

According to Compellingtruth.org, "In biblical times, a cornerstone was used as the foundation and standard upon which a building was constructed. Once in place, the rest of the building would conform to the angles and size of the cornerstone. In addition, if removed, the entire structure could collapse." Throughout many Scriptures in the Bible, Jesus is referred to as the Cornerstone of the Christian faith. Jesus as the Messiah is prophesied in Isaiah, the Psalms and other Books and then is directly identified as the Cornerstone throughout the New Testament.

Ephesians 2:19-22 reveals to us that Jesus is the cornerstone of our faith, "Now, therefore, you are no longer strangers and foreigners, but fellow citizens with the saints and members of the household of God, having been built on the foundation of the apostles and prophets, Jesus Christ Himself being the chief cornerstone, in whom the whole building, being fitted together, grows into a holy temple in the Lord, in whom you also are being built together for a dwelling place of God in the Spirit."

Scripture lays forth the "plumb line" of God for us. Plumb line is defined by Merriam-Webster as, "a line directed to the center of gravity of the earth: a vertical line." Scripture tells us that Jesus, as the cornerstone of our faith, is the measure of justice and righteousness for our lives. Isaiah 28:16-17 illustrates this truth, 'Therefore thus says the Lord God: "Behold, I lay in Zion a stone for a foundation, a tried stone, a precious cornerstone, a sure foundation; whoever believes will not act hastily. Also I will make justice the measuring line, and righteousness the plummet.'

This plumb line of justice and righteousness helps keep our lives in line with God's truth and keeps us from viewing truth from moral relativity according to the cultural shifts of our day. Truth does not change and it is not relative, nor does it shift with how the world spins it. Anything we think we hear from God that contradicts His word is not accurate. Everything in the spirit must be measured against Scripture so that we don't become deceived. As Christians, we need to have a balance of both the Word of God and the Holy Spirit in our lives.

Keep in mind as you're reading Scripture that some of the Bible is documentary and some is commentary. In some parts, God is just recording what happened historically and in other parts He is giving His heart over a matter. For example, in the Old Testament when King David and others had many wives and concubines, that was not the heart of the Father for David or for any of the women. God was merely documenting history by recording the details. God works toward bringing mankind into maturity as soon as He can. God spends many years preparing Moses to be a deliverer to the Israelites who are held captive in Egypt. One day it is fine that Moses' son has not been circumcised. The next day, actually as Moses is on his way to challenge Pharaoh, God confronts Moses over his lack of circumcising his son and wants to kill him for this egregious sin. Fortunately, Moses' wife Zipporah intervenes and circumcises the son and God relents. (Exodus 4:24-26) This story speaks of a principle in God that when you're about to be promoted on assignment, it's necessary to repent of any sin in your life. God always wants us to be walking in righteousness, but it's particularly important not to give the enemy any open doors of access to you as you're moving into the more.

Ephesians 6:17-18 tells us that the word of God is the sword of the Spirit in the armor of God, "And take the helmet of salvation, and the sword of the Spirit, which is the word of God; praying always with all prayer and supplication in the Spirit, being watchful to this end with all perseverance and supplication for all the saints."

Psalms 103:20: "Bless the Lord, you His angels, who excel in strength, who do His word, heeding the voice of His word." This verse gives us keys to the spiritual realm. When we declare God's written word found in Scripture or declare a prophetic word, angels are set on assignment to bring the word to pass. They listen for people to declare the word of God to charge them with their next mission. Our spoken words are powerful. "Death and life are in the power of the tongue," Proverbs 18:21. The reason our words are so powerful is that our positive words empower angels to work on our behalf and our negative words empower demons to create assignments of death against us and others.

PRAYER ACTIVATION

Ask the Lord if there are any demonic assignments you need to cancel on your behalf because of negative words you've spoken or have been spoken over you. If so, you can pray through it like this, "I cancel any assignment of death or destruction over my life and cancel the harvest of the negative words now, in Jesus name." Ask the Lord if there are any assignments He wants to create for you on your behalf through declaring the word of God over your life. If so, declare them now. Journal any revelation here.

_____
_____
_____
_____
_____
_____
_____
_____

Hebrews 4:12: "For the word of God is living and powerful, and sharper than any two-edged sword, piercing even to the division of soul and spirit, and of joints and marrow, and is a discerner of the thoughts and intents of the heart."

We had an interesting occurrence with Hebrews 4:12 in our house in Michigan. We had an artist paint a mural in both of our daughters' rooms with Scripture. Our oldest daughter's room had a gorgeous apple blossom tree with a swing and other beautiful scenes throughout the room. Our youngest daughter's room had Scripture about God loving her with an everlasting love and how He provides sweet sleep to His beloved. Both rooms, as well as the rest of the home, were peaceful, lovely, and full of the Presence of God. When we put the house up for sale to move to Redding, California, I asked the Lord if we could sell it quickly and not show it much because I was busy with three young children at home. We had a lot of showings and began to get reports back from our realtor that some of the people coming through had strong reactions to the house, especially the bedrooms. They reported "hating" the bedrooms and a few ran out of the house! That was surprising to us because the bedrooms had Pottery Barn decor and were so pretty. I asked the Lord about it and He told me that they were experiencing Hebrews 4:12. The Scripture on the walls and the Presence of God were showing them that without Jesus as a Savior they were lost and that He is the Way, the Truth, and the Life. After that revelation, I told Him He could use our home to witness to as many people as possible. God took me at my word because we ended up showing the home 34 times before it sold.

God always prepares you with a word or a Scripture or a dream before a challenge. What He gives you will be your encouragement and your key for fighting through the battle. A few weeks before my liver failed in 2003, I read the book of Job. And my husband read the book of Job a month before our financial battle began. For both of those trials, the message from God was that it was the enemy stealing and that we could trust that the Lord would restore. We held onto God's goodness and faithfulness to us during both of those seasons.

Weighing & Responding to Prophetic Words

The process for weighing/responding to prophetic words is fairly straightforward but can require a lot from a person. When you receive a word either personally from God directly to you, or in the form of a prophetic word given to you, Scripture says to test the word. You test it by witnessing to it. In Old Testament times, because only prophets and kings heard the voice of the Lord through the Holy Spirit, if they delivered an inaccurate word through an ulterior motive, the consequence for them was death by stoning. God spoke clearly to the prophets in the Old Testament. They plainly knew what God was saying. The people receiving the word were not able to witness to it or test it because they didn't have the Holy Spirit indwelling them. In New Testament times, we each have the Holy Spirit, so it is the responsibility of the receiver of the word to test it through interacting with

God. We have to learn to hear the voice of God and the multiple ways He speaks. It's not easy the way it was in the Old Testament. We have to learn through relationship with Him His heart and His ways. We learn through practice and experience what He's saying, and what the interpretation and application are. We make mistakes learning to prophesy. Fortunately, we're not given the same consequence of stoning that the prophets of old were. Also, our understanding that the one receiving the word is the one responsible to witness to it and pray into it gives the one prophesying the freedom to develop his or her prophetic gift through practice. As we're faithful to practice, we can grow into being able to prophesy accurately all manner of words of knowledge, timing, direction and other things. We owe the world an encounter with the One who loves them beyond measure. Accurate, powerful prophetic words are a tool for showing someone how loved they are by God. God deeply desires to speak to pre-believers through His believers. Especially when we're ministering in the marketplace or public square, we have to be skilled at quickly receiving and delivering a prophetic word. We don't have the luxury of a forty- minute worship set, low lights, and a company of worshippers to prepare us to deliver a prophetic word in public. In our quest to obey Jesus by discipling nations and preaching the Gospel through the world, we'd better all be competent in our ability to accurately and quickly deliver prophetic words.

If you're a feeler, an accurate word will make you feel peace in the diaphragm area of your upper abdomen. Even if your soul doesn't like the word or the word scares you, check your spirit for a witness. Also, a word may be partially correct. If you can sort through it either by feeling or by asking God about it, you can take what's accurate and discard what's not. Often if a word is not right, it's in the area of timing or application. If I can sort through a word with confidence, I'll keep the parts that apply. If not, I'll ask God to give the word to me again because I value what He has to say. A word that's not right will feel like a "thud" in the same abdomen area.

And you'll feel a "check" in your spirit. Another reason words aren't accurate is if the revelation goes through a "filter" the person has. If you can identify the filter, you can sort the word for a correct interpretation. For example, if they personally have a heart for a certain people group or socioeconomic class or nation, they may filter all their words through other people ministering to the same people. If you re-listen to the word with understanding of a potential bias, you may be able to hear what God is communicating to you personally. Another helpful way people witness to words is through "God goose bumps". When I get God bumps, I'll know God is saying that what was just said or thought is correct. Especially, if the God bumps are full body. Often, feelers can immediately witness to a word or not and therefore, it doesn't require any more time for them.

If you're not a feeler, you'll dialogue with God about the word and He'll respond in the ways He speaks to you personally. Usually people who aren't feelers will "hear" from God or He'll show them a picture and then the interpretation.

Once you test the word and are satisfied that it's an accurate prophetic word for you, then the next step is to ask God what you're to do about it and what the timing of it is. Again, if you're a feeler, you may know or feel what you should do to partner with the word. Or, you may have a check that you're not to do anything right now. God may or may not show you anything at this point but it's important for your stewarding process to inquire of the Lord. If He doesn't show you anything, wait on Him to unfold the word.

At this point in the process, it's helpful to tell your spouse or your best friend or your Ignite group leader or your pastor about the word and ask them to pray into it with you. Please don't make radical life decisions regarding marriage, moving or job changes based upon a prophetic word. Your interpretation and application of the word could be inaccurate. God will confirm major life decisions through telling you directly, through multiple prophetic words, and through counsel with trusted leaders. Once you're confident in what the Lord is saying, please, with wisdom and faith, take action.

Most prophetic words begin a process to prepare you to be the person capable of walking out the word. Psalm 105:19 illustrates this concept, "Until the time that his word came to pass, the word of the Lord tested him." Your words will test you and grow you. Often it seems after a prophetic word, all hell breaks loose against you, and the opposite of what God said happens. The battle, using your prophetic word as a sword, gets the enemy out of your promised land and strengthens you in the necessary areas. Some people give up before birthing the promise. The bigger the promise, the longer the preparation time. Your faith and your belief and your character will all be tried during the process. If you keep believing and keep following God and take any important steps to defeat the enemy in your life, it'll come to pass.

PRAYER ACTIVATION

Take some time now to ask God if there are any prophetic words that may have been aborted that He wants to resurrect. Also, ask Him if there are any steps you need to take now for any of your prophetic words. Journal below.

_____
_____
_____
_____
_____

Annie Blouin

God's Voice

CHAPTER 8

SHIFTING ATMOSPHERES

As Believers, we have the ability and authority to shift a spiritual atmosphere to bring God's kingdom. The ability to feel atmospheres comes through the gift of discerning of spirits referenced in 1 Corinthians 12:7-11, "But the manifestation of the Spirit is given to each one for the profit of all: for to one is given the word of wisdom through the Spirit, to another the word of knowledge through the same Spirit, to another faith by the same Spirit, to another gifts of healings by the same Spirit, to another the working of miracles, to another prophecy, to another discerning of spirits, to another different kinds of tongues, to another the interpretation of tongues. But one and the same Spirit works all these things, distributing to each one individually as He wills." Discerning of spirits means you're able to differentiate between what the Holy Spirit and angels, the demonic spirits, and human spirits are doing. Ephesians 5:8-13 exhorts us to walk in the light, "For you were once darkness, but now you are light in the Lord. Walk as children of light (for the fruit of the Spirit is in all goodness, righteousness, and truth), finding out what is acceptable to the Lord. And have no fellowship with the unfruitful works of darkness, but rather expose them. For it is shameful even to speak of those things which are done by them in secret. But all things that are exposed are made manifest by the light, for whatever makes manifest is light."

Discerning of spirits is a gift of the Holy Spirit to help others around us who may not discern the spiritual atmosphere but are oppressed by it. Discernment operates either through "feeling" an atmosphere through your emotions or through "knowing" an atmosphere because of your thoughts. Spiritual atmospheres often determine what happens in them. For example, if there is an atmosphere of fear and anxiety, people who are in or come into the region will begin to experience fear and anxiety in their emotions and thoughts and may begin to think from a fearful perspective. An atmosphere can be as small as over a person or a single room or as big as over a city, state, or nation. Atmospheres will be anchored by either the angelic or the demonic. An atmosphere of innovation can cause people to have hope, to dream, and to design creatively. Worship creates atmospheres where people encounter God and begin to have their minds renewed to His perspective. Reconciliation can easily occur in an atmosphere of worship.

As Believers, we're responsible to carry our own atmosphere of Heaven with us wherever we go. It's often referred to as carrying our own "open heaven". Ephesians 2:6 tells us, "and (He) raised us up together, and made us sit together in the heavenly places in Christ Jesus,". Because we're seated in heavenly places even as we walk this earth, we're able to bring the atmosphere of heaven to earth and shift atmospheres. It's also essential to have a renewed mind, especially if you're sensitive in discerning of spirits. Romans 12:2: "And do not be conformed to this world, but be transformed by the renewing of your mind, that you may prove what is that good and acceptable and perfect will of God." If you don't have your mind anchored in God's word and His truth, feeling and hearing thoughts from atmospheres will shift you around. James 1:5-8 shares the truth of being anchored in God by saying, "If any of you lacks wisdom, let him ask of God, who gives to all liberally and without reproach, and it will be given to him. But let him ask in faith, with no doubting, for he who doubts is like a wave of the sea driven and tossed by the wind. For let not that man suppose that he will receive anything from the Lord; he is a double-minded man, unstable in all his ways."

The more spiritually sensitive you are, the more you need to be anchored in God's word. People who are strong in the gift of discerning of spirits often think they're going crazy because their emotions and thoughts can be all over the board from one minute to the next. I believe that a high percentage of people who are diagnosed with mental illness are really just people who see, hear, and feel in the spiritual realm without understanding. Romans 11:29 reveals, "For the gifts and the calling of God are irrevocable." Meaning that even unsaved people can be feelers and not know it is a gift or how to use it. God's purpose behind giving people gifts of discerning of spirits or the "feeler gift" is for them to perceive what is really going on in the spiritual realm that is subsequently driving the natural realm. Believers who understand their authority and their assignment can shift atmospheres and bring God's will to earth. The feeler gift is one of the most difficult gifts to bring to maturity. Until mature, the feeler can feel crazy. The key is understanding what are your own thoughts and emotions and what is in the atmosphere. Especially, if you still need heart healing, it can be hard to distinguish what's yours and what's not in an environment. Pursuing God, pursuing maturity, pursuing healing all help to bring the feeler gift to maturity.

Our natural emotional state with God should be peace and joy. It takes healing and maturity to get to that place, but that's how the mature Christian navigates life. Romans 14:17: "for the kingdom of God is not eating and drinking, but righteousness, peace and joy in the Holy Spirit." A key to knowing if something you discern is yours, whether it's in the atmosphere, or both, is checking your thoughts and emotional state before entering a new room, or house or store. If you're peaceful one moment and you go somewhere new and feel anxious, you came under an environment. Just because you feel an atmosphere shift does not mean that you have a responsibility to do anything about it. Often, if you try, you'll get into a battle that the Lord didn't intend for you. Corporations carry atmospheres based on their culture and identity. When you walk into one of their stores, you'll feel the atmosphere that the corporation carries. They can range from positive to neutral to negative. If I'm struggling emotionally and I still need to shop and run errands, there are certain stores that I'll avoid because that day I won't have the fortitude to maintain my own atmosphere. There are other stores that carry such hope and a positive atmosphere, I'll go in just to browse and be encouraged. Driving down the road, especially on a long road trip, can be very tiring because of the all the atmospheres a feeler can discern. If you're a strong feeler, build in rest times and understand how to care for yourself well.

The feeler gift is one of the most powerful of all spiritual gifts. A friend of mine who is a school teacher asked me to come into her school at the end of the year to discuss some dynamics that were concerning. When I walked in, I immediately felt a demonic spirit in the classroom and in the hallway. My friend is not a feeler and was not aware of the atmosphere, but she was definitely aware of the struggles they were having because of the unseen realm. I listened to her concerns and told her what I was discerning. We prayed together and asked God for His solution in shifting the atmosphere. We took authority over the atmosphere and shifted it to be inline with Heaven. The following year, she reported that the students and the other teachers all had a dramatically better year.

When you're aware of atmospheres, always ask God what your responsibility is, if any, in shifting atmospheres. Some of what you pick up won't be for you to do anything with. The majority of the time the Raleigh, North Carolina, region feels hopeful, energetic, innovative, industrious, and peaceful to me. The Triangle region also carries a spirit of religion and sexual lust. Both are in the process of being displaced by what Believers are doing in the area. The demonic principalities of religion and lust do not need to be addressed, nor is it safe to engage them. As Believers bring the Holy Spirit to the area and the gifts of the Holy Spirit and purity, the demonic will lose its foothold and will leave. There are times when the demonic will launch an attack into the atmosphere of a region and oppression will set in for a few days. It often feels like major anxiety, depression, and hopelessness that agitates feelers. Feelers who don't know it's in the atmosphere, or who still need some healing in those areas, will isolate and withdraw and basically suffer through the attack. It's important for feelers to have a network of other known feelers so that rather than withdrawing, they can check with each other if something is in the atmosphere. Then, check with God about the strategy to shift it. Usually, what I do is release the opposite over the entire region. If I discern fear, I'll release the perfect love of God because 1 John 4:18 tells us, "There is no fear in love; but perfect love casts out fear, because fear involves torment. But he who fears has not been made perfect in love." I have a feeler friend who lived about thirty minutes away from me on the opposite side of Raleigh. She contacted me one-night checking with me about the atmosphere. We were both discerning the same things so we agreed to release peace to the city. Less than a minute after we prayed, we both felt the city shift into peace. The shifting of atmospheres is one way that Believers disciple nations. John 1:5 talks about Jesus coming into the world as Light, with power to shift darkness, "And the light shines in the darkness, and the darkness did not comprehend it."

Practical Tools

The first thing for people who carry the discerning of spirits gift is to connect their discernment to the Holy Spirit. The Holy Spirit asked me years ago if I wanted to connect my discernment to Him. Instantly, I felt afraid that I wouldn't be able to protect myself anymore. After having that thought, the Holy Spirit asked me again if I wanted Him to protect me or if I wanted to continue defending myself. I had grown up using discernment to navigate some scary situations. I knew the right answer was to allow Holy Spirit to direct my discernment. I told Him I needed help trusting Him and healing for my heart, and I told Him I wanted to connect my discernment to Him. He then showed me that when discernment is used in self protection, the enemy uses it as an inroad to bring fear to the person. After I prayed to connect my discernment to the Holy Spirit, my feeler gift quieted way down. I then only noticed a fraction of what I had prior. It also took a few months to recalibrate so that fear was not mixed in with my discernment.

PRAYER ACTIVATION

If you've never connected your discernment to Holy Spirit before, I invite you to pray this. "Holy Spirit, I connect my discernment to You. I ask You to show me only what You'd have me see, feel, know, hear. Please properly calibrate my discernment gift. Thank You." Journal any thoughts here and today's date.

_____
_____
_____
_____
_____
_____
_____
_____
_____

If I discern something in an atmosphere, I don't intentionally look to see if it's also connected to or is harassing a person. Ephesians 6:12: "For we do not war against flesh and blood, but against principalities, against powers, against the rulers of this age, against spiritual hosts of wickedness in the heavenly places." If I have authority in the area, I'll check with God about releasing the opposite. If I don't feel a check from Holy Spirit, I'll release what He's doing. For example, if I discern control, I'll often release self-control into the atmosphere.

If I do see something and it's connected to someone and it's reaching out to me to either bring torment or try to get agreement, I can say aloud, under my breath, "I see you and I send you back." Dawna DeSilva at Bethel taught us that tool for ministering in the healing rooms. The demonic can't hear your thoughts, so you have to command the demonic aloud to get it to obey. If that was the root of what I felt, I won't feel it anymore. The person also may become more aware of the spirit, personally, and seek to get free from it.

We're all on a journey to maturity and freedom. Thankfully, the Lord and people help us along the way and don't reject us for being in process. If I have a relationship with someone who isn't yet free from a demonic spirit that interjects itself into the conversation at times, I'll pray "Everything between us must filter through the Cross of Jesus Christ." That allows our relationship along the journey to be full of love and fun and allows us to see each other as Christ sees us. Also, if I'm struggling with fear or something else, I'll pray the same prayer so that what I say isn't tainted through fear to hurt anyone until I'm free from it.

Apostles and apostolically gifted people can help prophetic people by pushing out their apostolic covering over their home, their church, their city. When the apostles live with their covering extended, people are able to access peace, prophetic revelation, and God easier. If you believe you carry an apostolic gifting, ask God to help you intentionally push out your covering.

Prophet Jennifer Eivaz from Turlock, California says, "Drama is usually a sign of demonic interference." When things are stirred up and crisis' happen, be sure to take authority over any demonic meddling. We want to focus on bringing God's kingdom to earth and not have our efforts thwarted, which means we need to be vigilant to take authority in order to move forward gaining fruit. I pray over my home, over a hotel room, over a room when I teach by taking authority. I usually say something like this, "I plead the Blood of Jesus over this room/house. I command anything that's not of the Lord to leave and not return. Holy Spirit, I welcome You to flood this place and ask for angels to bring your kingdom."

If you're feeling a lot and you're overwhelmed, cleaning your physical environment like your home, car, or room, can help bring peace to the chaos you feel. Another helpful thing is to incorporate routine into your life. I like going to the same restaurants, eating the same food especially when I'm feeling a lot in the atmosphere. Not having to deal with new situations assists my internal world in remaining peaceful. Writing down the things in your head can also free up some emotional head space. For example, making a to do list so that you don't have to remember it helps. Journaling with God and asking Him how He sees you and your world can help.

Prophetically Leading Worship

Worship leaders who take authority over the room before the worship set begins are able to bring the people into the presence of God much faster. We've all experienced differing degrees of the presence of the Holy Spirit in meetings and at home in our quiet time with the Lord. We know that God desires to be with us. Psalms 22:3 tells us, "But You are holy, enthroned in the praises of Israel." Our worship to Him invites more of Him in our midst. Isaiah 6:1: "In the year that King Uzziah died, I saw the Lord sitting on a throne, high and lifted up, and the train of His robe filled the temple." Worship leaders have the opportunity to host His presence for the congregation and can be intentional hosts. Prophetically leading worship has lots of components, more than just playing an instrument and singing.

Practical steps to prophetically leading worship include:
1. Take spiritual authority over a room.
2. Can't go in public worship where haven't gone in private intimacy with God.
3. You're inviting others into your private intimacy and taking them into the Throne Room with you.
4. You're prophetically hosting an atmosphere. Just like when you host a party, you're paying attention to the party atmosphere and serving your guests well. Symbolically refilling drinks, serving more food, leading the conversation so that they have a great time.

5. Listening to the Lord as you lead and following His direction. Paying attention to what is happening in the Throne Room and matching that mood. May need to alter set list as leading so that you stay with the anointing and the wave of the Spirit.
6. High praise carries a breaker anointing that welcomes the Spirit of God, which then leads to a sweet intimate worship atmosphere. Almost like starting fast dancing at a dance party and then leading into slow dancing.
7. Prophetic hosting can be very tiring because you have to keep track of all the details in the room. For example, you're the leader of the people, the leader of all the musicians, you're paying attention to any demonic activity that needs to be taken care of, you're trying to release the frequency that Heaven is releasing at that moment, you're paying attention to what the Angels are doing, you're trying to release the Sound that Heaven is releasing at that moment.
8. One person has to be the designated spiritual leader on the team who is hosting all of this. There can't be a battle over who that is and also can't be no one in that position. The lead vocalist isn't always the one spiritually hosting. Ideally they are, but if they don't step into it, there is a noticeable vacuum in the atmosphere that the demonic realm often takes advantage of. Those sets feel like chaos with very little presence of God.
9. Can designate worship intercessors to take care of some of the details so that it all doesn't fall on the leader's shoulders.
10. It really helps to have someone who is a feeler/strong discerner lead because the others don't feel the atmosphere shifts.
11. Be sensitive to dialoguing with God about necessary adjustments during the set.
12. Ask Him ahead of time what He wants to release and how through your set.

13. Also, if the congregation doesn't know the songs really well, it can turn into more of a concert where the people don't enter into the Presence as strongly. It may be a little boring as a musician to play the same songs over and over, but it can help the people engage more easily with God.

It's important to "brush yourself off" after ministering or working. It can help restore your energy and remove any potential demonic assignments or backlash. My husband or a friend will brush me off after teaching or ministering and then my body and my emotions don't need as much recovery time. What this looks like practically is literally my husband brushing off my upper back with his hands for a few seconds and praying aloud, "I brush you off. I command anything that's not of the Lord to leave and not return." Then he'll lay his hand on my back and pray for a fresh infilling of the Holy Spirit, saying, "Holy Spirit, please fill Annie with Your Spirit and Your Presence and Your perfect love." The entire process takes 10-15 seconds and is remarkably refreshing.

The Lord has shown me some pain or ailments on the physical body that can be connected to areas needing ministry. In a dream, I saw trauma can reside in the upper trapezius muscles on the back. "Brushing off" the trauma from that area and praying for a Holy Spirit infilling can heal trauma.

There's a prophetic spot on the back where the lower and middle trapezius muscles connect to the inside of the shoulder blade. If that spot hurts, on either side of the back, it can indicate the person's voice is stopped up. If they pray, make declarations the Lord wants them to make, or pray in tongues the pain should release.

Bladder issues, especially hyperactivity in the bladder, can result from unforgiveness towards an earthly father or a needing to release the earthly father from expectations he isn't capable of fulfilling. Forgiving and releasing the father from judgments and expectations can bring healing and relief to the bladder.

The pelvic area low in the abdomen can be an area where emotional insecurity resides in the body. It can eventually lead to reproductive organ pain or lower gastrointestinal issues. Emotional insecurity can also reside as a subcortical pain under the sternum in the chest area.

Laying hands on these areas and asking God to heal insecurity and bring His perfect peace and security can bring resolution to the body and bring security to the heart.

God's Voice

CHAPTER 9

NEXT MOVE OF GOD

The next move of God will be filled with more power, more love, and more of God than anything we've yet seen in our lives. There is a tension between "Now and Not Yet" in the Kingdom. We can have everything that God promised us through the Cross. Jesus said in John 14:12 that we'd do even more than He did when He walked the earth, "Most assuredly, I say to you, he who believes in Me, the works that I do he will do also; and greater works than these he will do, because I go to My Father." And yet, we're not fully walking in all of that corporately. There's more. There's so much more! We don't want to miss out on or disqualify the current move of God that's happening at CTF and around the world. The revival that began in 1994 in Toronto carrying the Father's heart is still going strong around the world. Bethel Church has stewarded God's Presence and walks in healings and miracles. However, every previous revival in history ended at some point but it doesn't have to. Nor is it the heart of God for revival to end. The Body of Christ is consciously stewarding this revival to pass it on through generations and see the continued increase of His kingdom on earth. Isaiah 9:6-7 prophesies, "For unto us a Child is born, unto us a Son is given; and the government will be upon His shoulder. And His name will be called Wonderful, Counselor, Mighty God, Everlasting Father, Prince of Peace. Of the increase of His government and peace there will be no end, upon the throne of David and over His kingdom, to order it and establish it with judgment and justice from that time forward, even forever. The zeal of the Lord of hosts will perform this."

The level of miracles and revival that we currently see should increase. As we're faithful with what God has already given us, He'll give us more to accomplish our assignment of discipling nations and preaching the Gospel to the ends of the earth. For revival to transform nations, we need it to become a cultural reformation. This move of God has to move further outside of the walls of the church, into the marketplace and every area of society.

There are many issues in people's lives that need miracles and many societal concerns that need a touch from God and a foundational reform. God gave the prophet Ezekiel a key in Ezekiel 37:1-14, 'The hand of the Lord came upon me and brought me out in the Spirit of the Lord, and set me down in the midst of the valley; and it was full of bones. Then He caused me to pass by them all around, and behold, there were very many in the open valley; and indeed they were very dry. And He said to me, "Son of man, can these bones live?" So I answered, "O Lord God, You know." Again He said to me, "Prophesy to these bones, and say to them, 'O dry bones, hear the word of the Lord! Thus says the Lord God to these bones: "Surely I will cause breath to enter into you, and you shall live. I will put sinews on you and bring flesh upon you, cover you with skin and put breath in you; and you shall live. Then you shall know that I am the Lord."'"' So I prophesied as I was commanded; and as I prophesied, there was a noise, and suddenly a rattling; and the bones came together, bone to bone. Indeed, as I looked, the sinews and the flesh came upon them, and the skin covered them over; but there was no breath in them. Also He said to me, "Prophesy to the breath, prophesy, son of man, and say to the breath, 'Thus says the Lord God: "Come from the four winds, O breath, and breathe on these slain, that they may live."'" So I prophesied as He commanded me, and breath came into them, and they lived, and stood upon their feet, an exceedingly great army. Then He said to me, "Son of man, these bones are the whole house of Israel. They indeed say, 'Our bones are dry, our hope is lost, and we ourselves are cut off.' Therefore, prophesy and say to them, 'Thus says the Lord God: "Behold, O My people, I will open your graves and cause you to come up from your graves, and bring you into the land of Israel. Then you shall know that I am the Lord, when I have opened your graves, O My people, and brought you up from your graves. I will put My Spirit in you, and you shall live, and I will place you in your own land. Then you shall know that I, the Lord, have spoken it and performed it." Says the Lord.'" This vision for Ezekiel shows the vital role of God's people praying, prophesying and declaring and the resulting life and transformation.

What does this look like today in our world? The Body of Christ has been praying for decades for numerous cultural changes. I believe we'll see Rowe v Wade overturned in our day because of all the prayer that has gone forth. However, it's not enough to just change the law because we can't legislate morality. The Body of Christ has to be prepared to mother and father practically through adoption all of the babies who will be born when the law changes and also mother and father the mothers and fathers who find themselves with unplanned pregnancies.

I also believe we're seeing changes in government, not just in the United States but around the world, because of all the prayer that's gone forth. Just like natural birth is messy, the birthing of new governments can be disordered. Corruption has been exposed in the United States government and also in Hollywood recently. For decades, young women and boys have been preyed upon by predators in the entertainment industry. The recent exposure of Bill Cosby, Harvey Weinstein, and others has to do with the Body of Christ praying. The prayers allow the demonic strongholds that anchored the sexual predatory behavior to be uncovered. As the Body continues to pray it all through, righteous foundations can be established. Just like in Ezekiel, if he'd stopped praying, the miracle would have ended. He had to pray it all the way through to see the fullness of it manifest. Lou Engle's organization of *The Call* has prayer warriors who've accomplished mighty acts of cultural transformation. *Awaken the Dawn* which was held in October 2017 in Washington D.C. was a march for women's equality and women's voices being empowered. Simultaneously, women in Hollywood were empowered to speak out against the sexual atrocities they endured in working in that industry. Coincidence? No. We need to continue to prophesy that righteous foundations would be established in Washington, D.C., in Hollywood and in the other five spheres of influence in America and throughout the world.

On God's agenda for this next move of God is the empowering of women. We're seeing some of that beginning now. Women comprise over half of the world's population and are the largest group of oppressed people statistically. Women in the United States and the Western world have much more equality with men than do the majority of the women around the world. In 2011, I heard Graham Cooke speak at Bethel Church's Piercing the Darkness Prophetic Conference. He preached one of the most significant messages on women I've ever heard. His main point was that the devil is petrified of women. Genesis 3:14-15 in the Amplified Translation speaks of the curse for the devil, 'The Lord God said to the serpent, "Because you have done this, you are cursed more than all the cattle, and more than any animal of the field; on your belly you shall go, and dust you shall eat all the days of your life. And I will put enmity (open hostility) between you and the woman, and between your seed (offspring) and her Seed; He shall [fatally] bruise your head, and you shall [only] bruise His heel."' The woman carries huge authority to enforce what Jesus paid for on the Cross. Therefore, the devil's strategy is to disempower women around the globe. Unfortunately, many sectors of the Church and of false world religions have partnered with the enemy towards achieving that goal. The enemy has attempted to take out half of the Army of God through a doctrine of demons in utilizing a few Scriptures taken out of context to keep women silent in the Church. If this is your belief, I challenge you to study how Jesus empowered women and commissioned them to bring forth the Gospel.

A harvest of souls in the Middle East and around the world is ready to take place. This mission field is on God's agenda for hundreds of millions of salvations in the near future. We're on the precipice of it now. There is much work to be done and many roles to fill. People need to be intercessors, missionaries for the Gospel and missionaries into every area of society to help transform nations. A movement of Saints as business people, government officials, medical workers, athletes, coaches, entertainers, scientists and others all need to be prepared to be placed by God into leadership roles in the 7 mountains. All of this will take lots of money to accomplish. If you're called to business or arts and entertainment, you're called to make as much money as you can to finance the Gospel and finance discipling nations through Reformation.

During this next move of God, the ability to prophesy will greatly expand. The level of words of knowledge that Shawn Bolz is courageously pioneering will become normal for those who prophesy. He's raising the entire water level of the Body of Christ. It'll take carrying the Father's heart, corporate faith and practice to be trusted with this outpouring of the prophetic but it's a crucial tool for the harvest and for reformation.

Sounds of heaven through music, art and creativity will be necessary tools for the Saints. If you're one of these, your personal intimacy and relationship with God will be the womb for this next sound to come forth.

Annie Blouin

I have a childhood friend who recently lost part of his leg in a motorcycle accident. I was grieved upon hearing the news and held him up in prayer during his recovery. One night, I had a dream. In the dream, I was praying for him and I saw and felt his leg begin to vibrate at the place where the limb was missing. I heard God say during the dream to watch this vibration, that the vibration is the beginning of the leg's regrowth. I told my friend in the dream and we watched together the creative miracle as his leg regrew. When I awoke, I asked God about it. He told me that this next move of Him would carry the miracle working power for creative miracles to be common. I messaged my friend, told him the dream and what God had said and to be expectant for his missing leg to regrow. Last summer, I visited Catch the Fire Toronto. While I was there, I went into their prayer room for a worship and prayer set. The entire time I was in the room, my whole body vibrated like I had seen in the dream. It was almost uncomfortable it was so powerful. As soon as I left the room and the building, the vibrations in my body stopped. When I asked God about it, He said that Toronto's prayer room is carrying the power now for creative miracles and soon not only will they see miracles like in my dream but it'll be available corporately worldwide.

Be expectant! We have wonderful things to look forward to as we walk with God!

PRAYER ACTIVATION

Ask God what else He has planned for this next move of God and ask Him specifically what your personal role will be.

_____
_____
_____
_____
_____
_____
_____
_____
_____
_____
_____
_____
_____
_____
_____
_____
_____
_____
_____

Annie Blouin

Suggested Reading List

The Bible

Everlasting Prophetic: Bridging Heaven to Earth
 by Annie Blouin

Everlasting Doors: When the Supernatural Penetrates American Politics
 by Annie Blouin

Forgiveness
 by John Arnott

Healed from Codependency
 by Melody Beatty

Loving Your Kids on Purpose
 by Danny Silk

Braving the Wilderness
 by Brene Brown

Silencing the Accuser
 by Jacqueline & Daniel Hanselman

The Seven Mountain Renaissance: Vision & Strategy through 2050
 by Johnny Enlow

ABOUT ANNIE BLOUIN

Annie Blouin teaches Prophetic Revelation at Catch the Fire Raleigh/Durham's School of Revival. She has keen insight into the supernatural and equips her students to prophesy and operate supernaturally with a sound Biblical foundation. Her heart is to see Revivalists influence every area of society with love and wisdom. She has been happily married to Joe for 22 years and they have three beautiful children who love the Lord.

Books by Annie Blouin are available at:
www.lifepresspublishing.com
www.amazon.com

www.ingramcontent.com/pod-product-compliance
Lightning Source LLC
Chambersburg PA
CBHW081236170426
43198CB00017B/2776